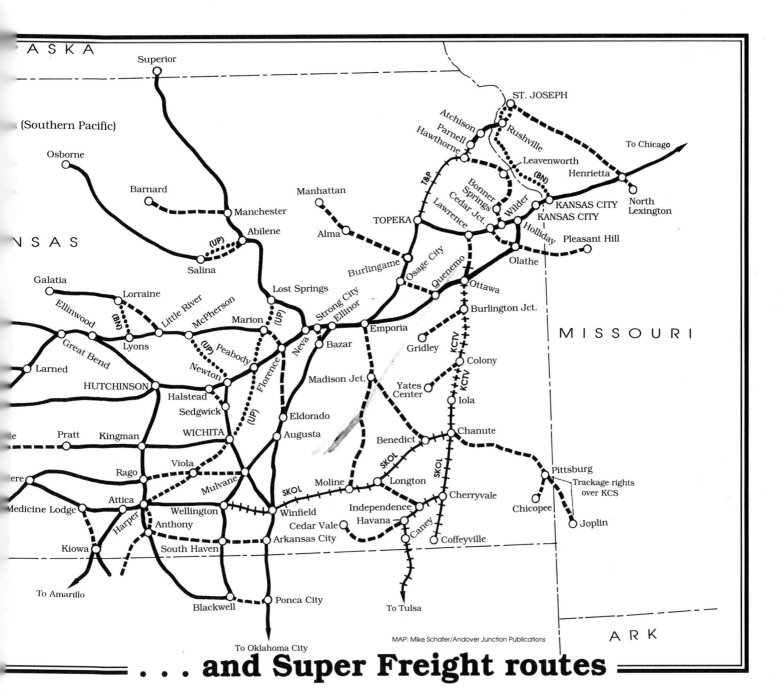

... and Super Freight routes

COLORADO AND KANSAS

See back endsheet for lines in Oklahoma and the Texas Panhandle

MAP: Mike Schafer/Andover Junction Publications

WHEAT LINES
and
SUPER FREIGHTS

Santa Fe In Color Series - Volume 2

Joe McMillan

WHEAT LINES AND SUPER FREIGHTS

Copyright © 1992 by Joe McMillan
Published By: McMillan Publications, Inc., Woodridge, Illinois
Book Layout and Design: Joe McMillan
End Sheet Maps: Mike Schafer, Zephyr Graphics & Editorial, Waukesha, Wisconsin
Dustjacket Design: Alan Barrett Graphic Design, Sacramento, California
Color Separations and Assembly: Jim Walter Color Separations, Beloit, Wisconsin
Printing: Winnebago Color Press, Menasha, Wisconsin
Binding: Zonne Bookbinders, Inc., Chicago, Illinois
Library of Congress Catalog Card Number: 92-90669
ISBN: 0-934228-17-5
First Printing: February 1992

Acknowledgements: A special thanks goes to the photographers whose work appears in this book. Appreciation also goes to Mike Blaszak who proofread the text and wrote the foreword, Keel Middleton and Steve Patterson for reviewing selected caption text, Vern and Mel Finzer for their aerial views, Mike Schafer for the excellent end-sheet maps, Jim Primm for his special help, and finally to the many Santa Fe folks who provided information. A big thanks to all of you!

Dustjacket and preceding page: EMD GP38 2339 at Medicine Lodge, Kansas on August 9, 1989. *Joe McMillan.* This page: SDFP45s 93 and 96 on Topeka Railroad Days excursion train at Lecompton, Kansas, August 31, 1991. *Jim Primm.*

Foreword
WHEAT LINES

Wheat, fields of it, stretching across the plains to the purple horizon, is the essence of Kansas. Each year, Kansas produces more wheat than any other state in America, and Kansas farms dominate the production of hard winter wheat, preferred for bread and other staples. The settlement of these plains and the development of these farms is the enduring legacy of the Santa Fe Railway in its native state of Kansas and the neighboring regions of Colorado and Oklahoma.

Home for millennia to enormous herds of bison, the plains also harbored the indigenous tribes known as Indians who hunted the beasts, ate their meat and wore their hides. The Spaniards who conquered the more developed peoples of the Americas in the Sixteenth Century made an occasional northward foray into the plains in search of the fabled riches of Cibola and Quivira, but they found only arid grasslands and hostile natives. Later, Spanish colonists advanced up the valley of the Rio Grande, through the territory of New Mexico, and established the City of the Holy Faith, Santa Fe, in 1610.

Far to the east, the English colonies, which had declared independence in 1776 as the United States, expanded in population and size. The young nation reached the edge of the plains beyond the northward bend of the Missouri River, at the western boundary of the new state of Missouri, in the 1820s. From there it was 800 dusty miles to Santa Fe, the northernmost outpost of the newly-independent nation of Mexico. Enterprising Americans soon discovered that simple goods like cloth, iron and tobacco, produced cheaply back East, could be sold to the remote New Mexicans at huge profits. Loading down capacious wagons with three tons of these commodities, the traders pointed their mules and oxen southwestward from the Missouri each spring, following their rutted paths back in the fall if the perils of drought, flash flood and Indian depredations had not done them in. The Santa Fe Trail, with its promise of adventure and riches, was born.

New Mexico became part of the U.S. following the Mexican War in 1848. Shortly thereafter, white settlement of the plains began in the Kansas (colloquially Kaw) River Valley stretching westward from the Missouri. Among the early immigrants was Cyrus K. Holliday, a young Pennsylvanian who had made some money in railroad construction back East. After playing a leading role in the development of the new town of Topeka on the banks of the Kaw some sixty miles from the Missouri border, Holliday became convinced that Kansas needed a railroad to develop the vast region beyond the watershed.

The Atchison and Topeka Railroad Company, it was called, under the charter drafted by Holliday in January 1859 and adopted by the original stockholders at Atchison, Kansas in September 1860. Through the efforts of Holliday and Senator S. C. Pomeroy, Kansas in 1863 obtained the promise of a substantial federal land grant to support construction of the railroad—but only if the railhead reached the western boundary of Kansas within ten years. To color the mundane corporate title with the romance of the old Trail, hopefully promoting the sale of stock, Holliday and his associates changed the firm's name to The Atchison, Topeka and Santa Fe Railroad Company on November 24, 1863.

The Santa Fe, as the company came to be known, did not meet with immediate success. The Civil War made raising capital difficult, and the location of the land grant in the unsettled, dry expanse of the western half of Kansas deterred potential investors.

In 1868, though, acquisition of reservation lands near Topeka from the Pottawatomie Indians finally gave Santa Fe an asset it could use to raise construction money. Ground was broken at a site near the present-day Topeka System Maintenance Terminal on October 30 of that year.

By March 1869 a three-span Howe truss across the Kaw to the Kansas Pacific (today's Union Pacific) was in place, and track materials began to flow to the railroad, advancing toward the coal-bearing lands near Carbondale. On April 26 Santa Fe invited about a hundred officials and local residents to enjoy an excursion from Topeka to Wakarusa, about twelve miles down the right of way. Rails had been laid only seven miles out, forcing the company to transfer its guests to horse-drawn coaches for the rest of the trip to the Wakarusa picnic grounds, but that inconvenience didn't inhibit Cyrus K. Holliday from delivering the rousing speech for which he is best remembered. Holliday emphatically predicted that the fledgling railroad would be built not only to old Santa Fe, but on to San Francisco, southward to the Gulf of Mexico, and east to Chicago and St. Louis. Onlookers who had watched the Santa Fe consume nine years building seven miles of track scoffed, but Holliday's prophecy ultimately would be realized—and as a Santa Fe board member till his death in 1900, Holliday survived to witness its fulfillment.

In July 1869 Santa Fe reached Carbondale; in July 1870 the railroad entered Emporia; and in July 1871 the company established the new town of Newton at the end of track, 137 miles from Topeka. Herds of Texas cattle off the Chisholm Trail at Emporia and Newton gave the Santa Fe its first traffic boom. The company expanded eastward as well, completing the line from Topeka to Atchison in April 1872. However, the ten-year deadline established by the 1863 land-grant legislation for completion of the railroad to the Kansas state line was drawing uncomfortably close. Santa Fe would have to lay track to the western border of Kansas—almost 300 miles from Newton—during the 1872 construction season in order to win the allotted federal lands.

Management accepted the challenge and ventured into the capital markets to raise the five million dollars required to fund the project. Starting in May 1872, track gangs proceeded from Newton to Hutchinson and then around the Great Bend of the Arkansas River, reaching Dodge City on September 19. The construction crew continued laying rails westward from "Dodge" across upward-sloping terrain in search of the unmarked state line. On December 22, amid cold rain and freezing temperatures, the foremen thought this all-important goal had been achieved and dismissed their workers to celebrate in the end-of-track tent town. A federal surveyor appeared shortly thereafter, though, to advise that the border was still four miles distant. Rounding up workers from the tents, the bosses ordered them to tear up what sidings existed on the hastily-built railroad and bolt the salvaged rails and ties into a four-mile extension which, on December 28, reached the state line and secured the land grant.

Now three million acres of property on either side of the track belonged to the Santa Fe. To assure long-term survival, Santa Fe had to sell its grassy domain to farmers who would provide steady agricultural traffic. Meanwhile, halfway around the world, the community of thrifty German Mennonites living in the Ukraine decided to depart for the religious freedom of the New World. Encouraged by a few members of their faith who had settled around Peabody, and by Santa Fe agents who quickly seized on their potential as colonizers of the land grant, some 15,000 Mennonites emigrated to Kansas between 1874 and 1883. The Mennonites brought with them the crop which would have the greatest impact on the Kansas economy—hard red winter wheat. Sown in the fall, nurtured during the cold, wet months of the winter and harvested in June, hard red winter wheat was resistant to drought, cold weather damage and the local pests which made short work of other crops. While corn production dominated Kansas agriculture in the early years, winter wheat became the staple crop after mills made the investments needed to grind this hard grain into high-quality flour.

To strengthen its weak western extension to the Kansas border, Santa Fe decided in 1875 to build onward toward Colorado and New Mexico, potential sources of coal, lumber, merchandise and tourist traffic. Reaching Pueblo in 1876, the railroad faced a choice. It could stop laying track and rely on the pioneering Colorado narrow-gauge route, the Denver & Rio Grande Railroad, to conduct its business in the Rocky Mountain region, or extend its own standard-gauge track to the sources of traffic. Under the aggressive leadership of former Burlington official William Barstow Strong, elected vice president in 1877 and president in 1881, Santa Fe elected to keep going. This decision led to the famous race with the Rio Grande for control of Raton Pass, which Santa Fe's crews won by just minutes on February 27, 1878. By 1880 rails had been laid over the Pass to Santa Fe itself, ending New Mexico's economic isolation and relegating the Trail to history.

More appealing than New Mexico as a traffic source, at least to contemporary rail managements, was Leadville, commercial center of a new mining region high in the Colorado Rockies which promised fabulous quantities of silver and other precious ores. From Pueblo, rails could be extended to Leadville only through the narrow confines of the Royal Gorge of the Arkansas River, a short distance upstream from Canon City. Rio Grande and Santa Fe clashed over this landmark as well. Though gangs employed by the rival railroads brandished small arms and committed occasional acts of vandalism against each other, most of the celebrated "war" for control of the Gorge was fought by attorneys in a variety of courts. The hostilities, which made engrossing newspaper copy but no money for railroad stockholders, finally ceased in February 1880 when Santa Fe agreed to let Rio Grande occupy the Gorge. The significance of Rio Grande's victory dwindled when the mines played out a few years later. By contrast, possession of Raton Pass paved the way for Santa Fe's eventual extension to California, which proved a far more valuable prize.

Back in Kansas, Santa Fe embarked on a course of building and buying branch lines to foster settlement of virgin lands and feed traffic to the main. The first branch had been constructed in 1872 from Newton to Wichita. In 1879 Santa Fe extended this branch southward to Mulvane, Winfield and Arkansas City.

Access to Kansas City was secured in 1875 after Santa Fe had taken over a separate railroad started by Cyrus K. Holliday to link that city to Santa Fe's rails at Topeka. Another independent railroad, chartered as the Leavenworth, Lawrence & Fort Gibson, but later known as the Southern Kansas, built from Lawrence to Coffeyville in the 1870s and then across the southern portion of the state to Wellington and Harper in 1880, invading territory claimed the year before by Santa Fe's extension of the Wichita branch. Santa Fe responded to this competitive threat by acquiring the upstart carrier on December 16, 1880. The parent road integrated the Southern Kansas into its route structure by building

a 14-mile connection from Olathe to Holliday, near Kansas City, in 1882 and a 56-mile line between Ottawa Junction and NR Junction, near Emporia, in 1883-84. These projects resulted in a direct rail route between Kansas City and Emporia, bypassing Topeka.

The branch-building campaign intensified in the mid-1880s as Santa Fe protected its territory against incursions from Missouri Pacific and Rock Island. Santa Fe's Chicago, Kansas and Western Railway subsidary, incorporated on November 21, 1885, constructed much of the new trackage, including the line which penetrates the fertile plains of north-central Kansas. From the junction with Santa Fe's main line at Neva, the CK&W built 114 miles northwestward to Concordia in 1887-88. Two branches were included, one from Ablilene to Salina (later extended to Osborne) and the other from Manchester to Barnard. Other CK&W projects included the Great Bend to Selkirk branch (later cut back to Scott City) and the cutoff from Hutchinson to Kinsley, bypassing Great Bend. Also in 1887, the Denver & Santa Fe Railway built a standard-gauge line from Pueblo to Denver, supplanting the trackage rights which Rio Grande had granted Santa Fe in 1882.

Railroading in the Lone Star state during the mid-1880s was firmly under the control of Southern Pacific's Collis P. Huntington and New York fiancier Jay Gould, who controlled railroads that would later become part of the Missouri Pacific. One significant line, the Gulf, Colorado and Santa Fe, was independent of these titans, being owned by investors in the port city of Galveston. With Gould in charge of the connecting railroads at its northern terminals of Dallas and Fort Worth, the GC&SF looked across the Indian Territory (now Oklahoma) to the Santa Fe for help. Strong was willing to meet the "GC" halfway, and work began.

The Southern Kansas, selected as the corporate platform for this project, secured two rights-of-way across the Indian Territory, one southward from Arkansas City and one southwestward from Harper. Strong then offered to buy the GC&SF if it would extend its line, at Santa Fe expense, from Fort Worth to Purcell, midway across the Territory, where it would be met by the Southern Kansas extension. The railroads met at Purcell on April 26, 1887, and Santa Fe commenced service across the Indian Territory within two months, although the GC&SF, due to the requirements of the peculiar railroad laws of Texas, survived as a separate Santa Fe operating unit until 1965.

Stong's southwestern thrust started from the end of the old Southern Kansas at Harper. Reaching the territorial border at Kiowa in 1885, the Southern Kansas extended to Waynoka by 1887 and on to Panhandle, Texas, by January 1888. Ultimately this line would be extended, by acquisition and construction, all the way to Belen, New Mexico, and would become Santa Fe's primary freight route.

Barely twenty years after turning its first shovelful of dirt on the banks of the Kaw in Topeka, the Santa Fe had, by 1889, matured from the vision of the pioneering, if eccentric, Holliday to a transportation colossus controlling some 7,400 miles of railroad lines which stretched from Chicago to California but were concentrated on the plains of Kansas. Unfortunately for William Barstow Strong, the man most responsible for turning Holliday's dream into reality, the railroad could not yet generate enough revenue to pay the interest on the enormous debt it had assumed to build and buy all these railroad lines, and the bankers controlling that debt forced him to resign in September of that year. A financial reorganization in the 1890s put the Santa Fe on a steady, conservative course for most of the Twentieth Century.

Although the great era of American railroad building was over, Santa Fe continued to expand as the new century unfolded. Addition of lines to the system was spurred by the settlement of the Indian and Oklahoma Territories, merged as the state of Oklahoma in 1907 and the advent of irrigation and improved dry land farming techniques, which made agriculture feasible in far western Kansas and eastern Colorado. Also, Santa Fe sometimes acquired other railroads to defend its territory against competition. New lines were built to Tulsa and across the eastern portion of Oklahoma's midsection during this period, as well as southwest of Dodge City. Santa Fe also bought the Hutchinson & Southern Railroad (Hutchinson to Ponca City) in 1899, the Denver, Enid & Gulf (Kiowa-Enid-Guthrie) in 1907, the Kansas Southwestern (Arkansas City to Anthony) in 1914, and the woebegone Kansas City, Mexico & Orient (Wichita-Alpine, Texas) in 1928. The purchase of the Orient was intended to keep Southern Pacific out of Kansas.

One important legacy of the Orient was an incomplete grade between Ellinor (near Emporia) and El Dorado, Kansas, which Santa Fe bought from its cash-starved neighbor after the Orient gave up ambitions of building to Kansas City in 1922. Completion of the line through the Flint Hills between these points in 1924 created an efficient freight cutoff between Chicago and Kansas City on the east, and California and Texas on the west and south, that was shorter than the old main routes via Newton.

The Santa Fe system serving the plains endured with relatively insignificant changes through the middle years of the Twentieth century. While most of the capital budget was lavished on the main lines, grain traffic remained critically important to the company's profitability, and direct service to country elevators on the web of branches covering the plains was the cornerstone of Santa Fe's marketing strategy. Steam power gave way to diesels in the Forties and Fifties, and covered hoppers displaced narrow-door boxcars starting in the Sixties, but local freights continued to prowl Santa Fe's branches to set out empties and gather loads as they had for decades.

The photographs in this book depict this relatively unknown, but still vitally important, network of Santa Fe lines serving Kansas, Colorado and Oklahoma, beginning in the 1960s and continuing up to the present. Much of the fascination of railroading in Kansas, as the case elsewhere on the plains, lies in the close relationship between the farmers, often descendants of the Mennonites and other immigrants of the pioneer era, and the railroad which brought their forebears to this productive land and still carries their harvest to market each year. During this period, however, the long-standing partnership between the Santa Fe and its country customers began to crumble under the increasing pressure of economic change, a tension which is reflected in the photos.

The rising cost of handling passengers, mail and less-than-carload freight, and of staffing stations in each town, forced the Santa Fe to begin eliminating these now little-used services in the Sixties. Regulatory and political opposition often turned these efforts into legal battles equalling the intensity, if not the notoriety, of the Rio Grande "wars" eighty years before. Indeed, Santa Fe succeeded in canceling the passenger tariffs applicable to most branch lines only as a result of the federal legislation that created Amtrak in 1971, though the accommodations had long since been restricted to the passenger-in-caboose variety. State resistance to station closings kept 105 depots in Kansas alone staffed with agents as late as 1980. In return for upgrading important stations to "Regional Freight Offices" equipped with computer terminals and fax machines during the early Eighties, Santa Fe obtained changes in state statutes which made it easier to eliminate country agencies. The company wasted little time closing these depots and razing most of the venerable station buildings as the decade progressed. No longer could the townsfolk saunter over to the depot to talk things over with the Santa Fe agent; by 1990 the nearest open agency was at the regional headquarters in Kansas City.

In some locations the survival of the railroad itself was threatened by declining traffic or deteriorating track. Many of the branches were equipped with rail which was adequate for the wooden boxcars of the 1880s but could not support the 100-ton covered hoppers of the 1980s. Santa Fe announced an 815-mile abandonment program in 1970 which claimed many branches during the ensuing decade. The pace of abandonments quickened during the Eighties as lines like the Manchester-Barnard and Chanute-Pittsburgh branches were eliminated. Meanwhile, the company's drive to increase profits during the decade led to discontinuance of regular local freight service on the remaining branches, replaced by trains running from branch to branch as needed from central points like Wellington as infrequently as once a week.

The surviving branch lines posed a dilemma for Santa Fe management as the Eighties drew to a close. Starved for capital investment during the past three decades, the branches would need costly rebuilding to remain in operable condition, but they did not generate anywhere near enough revenue to justify the expense. Politically, abandonment was out of the question since the farmers and on-line communities still relied on the lines to ship their grain. To extract its investment in these properties, Santa Fe elected to follow the contemporary industry trend by selling off the branches to short-line operators which could provide service at lower cost. The Garden City-Shallow Water line was sold in 1989; the lines radiating from Chanute were transferred in 1990, and the Orient was conveyed in 1991. In 1992 Santa Fe plans to sell a package of 830 miles of Kansas branches (Great Bend, Little River, McPherson, Larned, H&S, Wichita, Englewood and Medicine Lodge Subdivisions plus portions of the Salina and Hutchinson Subs) and will undoubtedly put other lines up for bid.

With the conclusion of the line sale program, Santa Fe's presence on the plains will be limited to its main lines and a few branches serving cities with large terminal grain elevators, like Salina and Enid. In place of the short, steam-powered freights of William Barstow Strong's day, Santa Fe operates scores of long intermodal consists flashing through the Flint Hills at seventy miles per hour behind red-and-silver Super Fleet locomotives and heavy unit trains carrying coal to electric power plants. The sod-busting, railroad-building age of the frontier is long past, and the railroad itself has reduced its role to a long-distance carrier specializing in high-volume transportation. Yet the 120-car trains ponderously rolling Kansas wheat out of the North Wichita yards toward the Gulf serve as a reminder that the plains and their denizens still rely on Santa Fe, and Santa Fe relies on them as well.

—— *Michael W. Blaszak*

January 1992

Santa Fe's mammoth Kansas City yard stretches five miles along the banks of the Kansas River. In addition to the Argentine diesel shop complex, now designated Argentine LMIT (Locomotive Maintenance Inspection Terminal), Argentine Yard features two large classification hump yards and all the associated receiving and departure tracks, a sizeable intermodal terminal, a car repair shop and even a Santa Fe-owned grain elevator. It's a busy place. Kansas City is also headquarters for the Eastern Region which stretches from Chicago south and west to Arkansas City, Kansas, St. Francis, Texas (near Amarillo) and La Junta, Colorado. The headquarters building, located off Kansas Avenue on the north side of the yard, houses the new Regional Operations Center (ROC) which dispatches the region's trains and crews.

Top left . . . The old AY Tower and yard office at the east end of Argentine Yard, photographed on May 26, 1973, was a classic structure. The building was later torn down and it's functions transferred to a new AY Tower on the south side of the tracks across from the old location. [See photo on page 187, Volume 1.] On September 17, 1991, this tower was closed and control of train and engine movements was assigned to a dispatcher in the ROC. *Bottom left* . . . The 500 series Fairbanks-Morse switchers were common fixtures at Argentine in the mid-1960s. On a bitter cold day in January 1965, the 562 drags brand new Chihuahua Pacific GP28 806 over the westbound hump. The orange unit will soon be en route to warmer climes. *Above* . . . Bicentennial SD45-2 5700 and three mates curve under the westbound hump on February 25, 1975 with train 100, the eastbound *Super C*, the company's hottest train at the time. These tracks were later removed with the construction of the "Fast Track" in 1990, a high speed short cut from the main line through the yard to the intermodal terminal on the north side of the complex. *Argentine LMIT sign and bottom left, Joe McMillan; AY yard office, Lee Berglund; above: Jim Primm.*

Left . . . Key Road viaduct (55th Street) passes over the west end of Argentine Yard at Turner, mile 7.1, and provides a nice vantage point from which to view trains. On July 12, 1989, the camera catches the first two "Super Fleet" SDFP45s (rebuilt FP45s) 102 and 101 backing down to their train. The two motors left Chicago earlier that morning on train 168. [See Volume 1, page 143.] From the Goddard Viaduct west of the shops . . . *above* . . . month-old GE DASH 8-40BW 517 pilots containers and trailers into the yard over the north Fast Track on November 10, 1990. The 4000 h.p. unit was one of 60 (500-559) delivered between October 12 and December 6, 1990. Twenty-three more (560-582) are due in mid-1992. *Below* . . . Santa Fe hosted a trio of Alco C-636 demonstrators in December 1969 and January 1970. The company wasn't impressed with the troubled units and they were quickly interchanged to the Southern Pacific, the next road scheduled to try them out. The demos eventually wound up on the Cartier Railway in Quebec as its 77-79. On January 12, 1969, the three gray and white units were at Turner preparing to leave on their fourth and final demo trip. *Left page: Jim Primm; above: Mark R. Lynn; below: Steve Patterson.*

Left . . . A rail tunnel in Kansas? Well, not exactly. The Santa Fe serves the Americold Corporation (formerly Inland Storage Distribution Company) on the south side of the main line at mile 9 between Turner and Morris. Two tracks penetrate the limestone cliffs to serve the loading docks of a huge underground cold storage facility. There are 913 feet of underground trackage in the west tunnel and 4,305 feet in the east. Santa Fe has served the facility since the early 1950s. GP7 2062 and mate pause outside the east portal on September 19, 1983. *Above* . . . Bicentennial 5702 leads a string of boxcars through crossovers from No. 4 main to No. 2 at mile 11 just west of Morris on September 5, 1976. (Where there are four or more main tracks, Santa Fe numbers them from left to right as viewed from a westward or southward train. Where there are three main tracks, they are designated south, middle and north; two main tracks are termed south and north.) *Below* . . . The Morris station, photographed on September 12, 1964, was located at mile 10.3, but was moved in the early 1980s to the grounds of the Agriculture Hall of Fame in Bonner Springs. The large bay window section of the station housed interlocking machinery for nearby crossovers until the coming of CTC in the 1950s. *Left page: David P. Oroszi; above: Jim Primm; below: Joe McMillan.*

There are four main tracks between Turner and just east of Holliday, a distance of 6.3 miles. *Top left . . .* GE U36C 8789 wheels westbound pigs on the No. 1 main, the "high line," at mile 12.5 on a winter day in February 1981, while a pair of eastbounds disappear in the distance on the No. 2 and No. 4 mains. *Bottom left . . .* Eight months later, C30-7 8141 moves a mixed consist along the Kansas River on the No. 3 main. Both photos were taken from the I-455 overpass, which was under construction at the time. Four days of torrential rains in July 1951 (on top of a very wet spring) caused the Kansas River to inundate large areas of western Missouri and eastern Kansas. Santa Fe's facilites in Kansas City were dealt a devastating blow on July 13th when water poured over the dikes flooding the yard to a depth of 22 feet at some locations. All transcontinental operations were suspended for ten days until the water receded and repairs completed. To prevent a recurrence, the railroad raised the No. 1 main in late 1951 and 1952 from mile 7.6 to 14.5, just west of Holliday. Dikes bordering the yard were raised and many other improvements were made, such as enlarging bridge openings. If such a flood reoccurs, the railroad will hopefully be able to maintain a route through the area.

Holliday, mile 13.5, is the junction with the Topeka Subdivision, formerly the First District. We will follow the Topeka Sub, and its branches, to Emporia, then return here and follow the Emporia Subdivision west (page 32). Topeka Sub mileposts begin at zero at Holliday. *Above . . .* CF7 2560 and two GP7s move the Tecumseh coal train westward at Wilder, mile 3.7, on August 10, 1976. The coal originates on the Union Pacific at Hanna, Wyoming and is interchanged to the Santa Fe at Kansas City. The train is often powered by older four-motor units. Tecumseh, named for a Shawnee Indian chief, is located on the Topeka Sub at mile 46.0. This photo was taken from Kansas Route 7. *Three photos: Jim Primm.*

Wilder was the junction with the Leavenworth District (Leavenworth Subdivision after October 27, 1985) until the last segment of the line was abandoned in February 1990. The branch was completed in November 1887 as the Leavenworth, Northern and Southern. It's rails headed northwest, crossing the Kansas River and the Union Pacific at Bonner Springs, and passed through Lansing and Leavenworth to Hawthorne on the Topeka-St. Joseph branch, a distance of 45.3 miles. The 23.3-mile Leavenworth-Hawthorne portion was abandoned in January 1961 and the Bonner Springs-Leavenworth section closed in September 1989. On September 12, 1964, members of the Topeka and Kansas City Chapters of the National Railway Historical Society teamed up to ride the Leavenworth District. Members rode drovers car D-932 coupled to caboose 2200R behind F-M 532. *Top left* . . . The switcher repositions the drovers car at Leavenworth for the return trip and later . . . *bottom left* . . . the short train pauses at Bonner Springs. At Wilder . . . *above* . . . the local waits as No. 11, the *Kansas Cityan* (Kansas City-Dallas), flashes by on the First District behind E3A 11. F-M 532 was renumbered 632 in March 1973 and sold to a scrap dealer in Vinton, Texas a year later. Drovers car D-932 is displayed at the Mojave River Valley Museum in Barstow, California. On June 7, 1980 . . . *below* . . . GP7m 2899 rumbles across a small trestle north of Bonner Springs en route to Leavenworth. This photo was taken from the Kansas Turnpike (I-70). *Left page and above: Joe McMillan; below: Jim Primm.*

Above . . . From an overhead vantage point at mile 11.3, the camera records the Topeka Sub local behind CF7 2584 slowing for a stop at De Soto, Kansas on August 25, 1979. Amtrak SDP40F 500 . . . *below* . . . powers a Kansas Governor inaugural special at mile 48.5 west of Tecumseh on January 8, 1979. That's Kansas Power & Light's Tecumseh plant in the background. *Top right* . . . SDFP45 101 and SDF40-2 5260 speed east under the Kansas Turnpike at mile 28.3 west of Lawrence with deadhead passenger equipment for Kansas City. It's August 31, 1989, and the train is returning from a Kansas Grain and Feed Dealer Association special in western Kansas. (See also page 66.) *Bottom right* . . . Santa Fe has participated in Topeka's annual Labor Day Railroad Days celebration by running passenger shuttles to nearby communities. In 1990, the trains ran between the celebration site at Pauline (mile 58) and Lakeview (mile 31.5) west of Lawrence. GP38-2s 2372 and 2374 (ex-TP&W) are two miles west of Lecompton on the first eastbound run of the day. *Two photos this page and top right: Jim Primm; bottom right: Dan Munson.*

For the Santa Fe Railway, Topeka is where it all began. From its humble beginnings in 1868, the company has always maintained a stong presence in the capitol city. For 101 years (1884-1985) the company's offices were located at 9th and Jackson Streets across from the state capitol. The General Office Building (GOB) was home for a number of system departments and the Eastern Lines, one of three operating regions or "grand divisions" on the railroad. (The Western Lines and Coast Lines, headquartered at Amarillo, Texas and Los Angeles, California, respectively, were the other two. A fourth grand division, the Gulf Lines, headquartered at Galveston, Texas, had been absorbed by the Western Lines in August 1965.) Each grand division was divided into several operating divisions. In 1967, for example, the company was comprised of 16 divisions. By early 1988, that number had been reduced to 10. On May 15, 1988, the railroad was reorganized into six divisions (Illinois, Kansas, Texas, New Mexico, Arizona and California) and the grand divisions were reduced to two: the Eastern Region headquartered at Topeka, and the Western Region at Los Angeles. In 1989, the two regions and their staffs were phased out, eliminating an entire layer of management. On August 15, 1990, the railroad was further reorganized into four operating divisions or "regions" (Eastern, Central, Western and Southern, with headquarters at Kansas City, Kansas; Albuquerque, New Mexico; San Bernardino, California; and Euless, Texas, respectively). Their managers now report jointly to the vice presidents of transportation and maintenance instead of a regional general manager. In 1985, the Topeka staff moved into a new office building at 920 Southeast Quincy. The beautiful building is home to a number of system departments such as payroll, accounting, operations research, management information systems and staff services.

Topeka was always a great place to watch passenger trains. *Left* . . . On September 17, 1964, the company ran a special train from Topeka filled with screaming teenagers going to a Beatles concert in Kansas City. E6As 15 and 14 grace the point of the four-car train. *Above* . . . Four years later GE U28CGs 355 and 353 ease No. 24 (formerly the *Grand Canyon*) out of Topeka. A deadheading full length dome car is coupled behind the units. Note the state capitol building above the second locomotive. The passenger station is located just out of the photo at left. *Below* . . . On July 20, 1968, No. 2, the *San Francisco Chief*, pulls away from the station. *Three photos: Joe McMillan.*

Above . . . On a pleasant evening in July 1968, No. 23 prepares to leave Topeka for the west behind U30CGs 400 and 404. The Chicago to Los Angeles train was scheduled to depart at 7:15 p.m. The passenger station, shown at the rear of the train at the left of the platform canopy, is the third station at this location. It was dedicated on April 3, 1949 and replaced a large ornate structure constructed in 1880 and 1881. The two buildings this side of the passenger station are former express buildings dating back to time of the former structure. Amtrak's *Southwest Chief* still stops here during the early morning hours. A portion of the Topeka Shops can been seen in the upper right corner.

Above . . . Santa Fe's 3000 class F-M H16-44s were a common sight on locals around Topeka for years. When this photo was taken on September 14, 1968, however, these three were the only ones operating, and in seven months they would be gone, too. On a snowy day in January 1987, Santa Fe C30-7 8155 . . . *below* . . . leads Red Rock coal empties, symboled C-RRTP, onto Union Pacific's main line in North Topeka. In a few minutes, the Santa Fe motors will cut off and return to Topeka. The UP will forward the train to Wyoming for another load. The coal train serves Oklahoma Gas & Electric's power plant at Red Rock, Oklahoma, 43 miles south of Arkansas City, Kansas on the Oklahoma Subdivision. The track angling off to the right is Santa Fe's Atchison Subdivision. *Left page and above: Joe McMillan; below: Andrew Taylor.*

Topeka is home to the railroad's largest shop complex: Topeka System Maintenance Terminal (SMT). The shops had their origin in 1878 when the fledging company purchased the idle facilities of the King Bridge Company in northeast Topeka. The shop has been enlarged many times over the years and its workers have built hundreds of steam locomotives and thousands of cars. Today the SMT focuses on reconditioning freight cars and repairing wrecked locomotives. A new locomotive paint facility went to work in 1990 converting Santa Fe red and yellow merger-painted units to traditional blue and yellow. In October 1991, Albuquerque's Central Work Equipment (CWE) shop was moved to Topeka. The CWE shop maintains the company's huge roster of maintenance of way machines—from pile drivers to spike pullers.

Middle left . . . Included in the thousands of cars built at Topeka were 3300 mechanical reefers of twelve classes. Here, brand new class Rr-86 cars roll out of the paint shop in July 1964, part of an order of 300 cars (50000-50299). In twenty years the company's mechanical reefer fleet would be phased out. The last two cars in revenue service were removed from the active list in April 1988. Topeka Shops has always maintained the company's business and passenger car fleet. On July 24, 1974 . . . *bottom left* . . . diner-lounge 1397 is being stripped prior to its conversion to track inspection car 89. The car—recently named *William Barstow Strong* in honor of Santa Fe's president from 1881 to 1889—was released in April 1975 and is often seen at the rear of today's business specials.

The Topeka Railroad Days celebration is always a exciting affair for area residents. Topeka's three railroads, Santa Fe, Union Pacific and Cotton Belt, display equipment at Pauline, 6.7 miles south of town. In addition to static displays, the Santa Fe also operates a passenger shuttle—usually with UP and AT&SF cars—for those attending the celebration. In 1990 . . . *top* . . . the Santa Fe displayed brand new GP60M 146, shown here at the diesel service facility coupled to a pair of EMD FT demonstrators sponsored by General Motors. The 146 had just been repainted to red and silver warbonnet after a brief stint in Maersk Lines blue for a TV commercial. Featured at the 1987 Railroad Days celebration was a gigantic two day auction of Santa Fe memorabilia. Thousands of items were sold, from china and drumheads to motorcars and railcars. Most of the artifacts were slated for a company museum that never materialized. *Top: Tom Chenoweth; all others: Joe McMillan.*

The Atchison District (Topeka-St. Joseph) was served for years by local trains 29 and 30 (1291 and 1292 after 1971) which originated at Emporia and made a round trip six days a week, usually on a overnight schedule. By 1989, the local was originating at Topeka and making daylight trips symbolled as LIL22. In 1990 and 1991, St. Joseph service was radically altered. On January 8, 1990, Santa Fe began operating over the First Subdivision of Burlington Northern's Nebraska Division between Kansas City and St. Joseph, serving Atchison via side trips over BN's branch from Armour. In the fall of 1991, the Santa Fe entered into a lease/haulage agreement with the Burlington Northern whereby BN leased the Rushville-Atchison portion of Santa Fe's St. Joe line to improve its access to Atchison. In exchange, BN handles Santa Fe traffic to Atchison and performs the necessary switching and interchange there. (The AT&SF, however, retains the right to operate its own trains to Atchison.)

Above . . . A year prior to the restructuring of Santa Fe's St. Joseph service, LIL22 approaches the U.S. Highway 24 overpass at mile 47.3 north of Topeka. (On June 25, 1991, the Atchison Sub between North Topeka and Parnell, 41 miles, was sold to the T and P Railway and in 1991 the segment was being served on an infrequent basis.) From Winthrop, Missouri (across the river from Atchison) to St. Joseph (Terminal Junction), Santa Fe exercised trackage rights over Rock Island's Atchison-Rushville-St. Joseph line, a distance of 20 miles. On May 1, 1984, the Santa Fe received the dilapidated line from the RI bankruptcy estate in a settlement, subsequently rebuilding it. *Below* . . . In September 1989, the Topeka-bound St. Joe local curves through Rushville, Missouri on former RI rails and crosses BN's First Subdivision. Santa Fe trains now use these BN rails to reach St. Joseph and BN trains use the Santa Fe tracks—by way of a new connection—to reach Atchison. *Right page* . . . Later that month, the LIL22 stops at the west end of the Atchison yard to set out and pick up. Union Pacific's ex-MoPac yard lies just to the left of the Santa Fe facility. MP 2162 and mate switch cars on an adjacent track. Note Santa Fe's Atchison freight house in the distant right. The ancient stone building was donated to the City of Atchison in December 1986 and is now a museum. *Five photos: Jim Primm.*

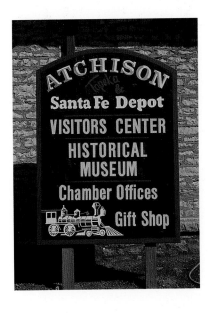

Santa Fe trains leaving Atchison for St. Joseph had trackage rights over the joint UP/BN bridge across the Missouri River. *Above . . .* B23-7's lead the St. Joe local over the river on October 7, 1989. This photo was taken from the parallel U. S. Highway 59 bridge. *Top right . . .* A month earlier, the local pauses at the east end while the bridge tender opens the gates after the passage of marine traffic. *Bottom right . . .* On a late afternoon in September 1968, Santa Fe train 29 prepares to leave St. Joseph's Terminal Yard for Topeka and Emporia behind GP7s 2851 and 2850 as a Chicago & North Western freight rumbles by on the way to Kansas City with ex-CGW F3A 4101-A (ex-CGW 150) on the point. *Above and top right: Jim Primm; bottom right: Joe McMillan.*

Santa Fe's first rails were laid on what is now the western portion of the Topeka Subdivision. After a connection with the Kansas Pacific in North Topeka was established, the new road built west with considerable speed. On June 28th, 1869, with 17 miles of track completed between Topeka and Carbondale, the "A. T. & S. F. R. R." opened for business. *Above* . . . Pauline, located at mile 57.3, is the first station west of Topeka. Its attractive depot was built in 1910 and closed in October 1982. During 1983, the building (minus the add-on baggage room) was moved to Topeka's Ward-Meade House and Park and restored. The station was photographed on March 28, 1976. *Below* . . . The westbound Red Rock coal loads (symbol C-TPRR) moves through Pauline in December 1988 behind two Santa Fe units and two UP's. Although some are replaced occasionally, semaphores were still common fixtures on the Topeka Sub in 1991. A trio of F-Ms and a GP7 lead No. 161 the westbound First District local through Carbondale . . . *bottom right* . . . on September 14, 1968. The area around here supplied locomotive coal to the Santa Fe in its infancy and local coal provided one of the first sources of revenue for the new railroad. *Top right* . . . Until it was removed from the property several years ago, the station at Burlingame, mile 77.0, was the oldest on the railroad. It was built in 1869 and while remodeled from time to time, it remained essentially as constructed. It's waiting room housed an interesting railroad museum for many years. Burlingame was the junction with the 33.8-mile Alma District and the A-B-A F-unit set will shortly head up the branch on its weekly trip. *Above: Jim Primm; below: James Mitchell; two photos right page: Joe McMillan.*

The Alma District was constructed in 1880 as the Manhattan, Alma and Burlingame Railway and was jointly operated by the Santa Fe and Union Pacific, an unusual arrangement in those days. The 56.4-mile line connected its namesake towns and provided farmers of the area with an outlet for their crops. The short-lived Alma-Manhattan segment was abandoned in 1898, but the rest of the branch survived until February 13, 1973. During its last years, the line was served weekly, usually on Wednesdays, by No. 162, the First District local. *Right* . . . You're looking out the fireman's window of H16-44 3013 as it approaches Mill Creek bridge at Alma on October 9, 1968. A few minutes later . . . *above* . . . No. 162's power disturbs the weeds as it bounces past the Alma depot after spotting a car. Alma was also on Rock Island's Kansas City-Herington main line (now the Cotton Belt) and Santa Fe occasionally interchanged a car to the Rock. *Top left* . . . The crew stops at Eskridge, mile 18, for lunch before continuing toward Burlingame. Eskridge was one of two open agencies on the branch at the time. *Bottom left* . . . Harveyville, mile 8.4, was the other open station, and on August 7, 1968, No. 162 approaches the station en route to Alma. Seventeen year old F7A 243C leads the local today. *Four photos: Joe McMillan.*

Above . . . We return to the Emporia Subdivision at Holliday, mile 13.4, in time to watch train 326 (Kansas City to Amarillo) roll west on the north main. The date is August 23, 1980. The track in the foreground is the Topeka Sub main track. *Below* . . . SD45 5561 and a pair of GEs speed mixed freight west on the north track at Craig, mile 18.6, on June 26, 1976. As a B&B gang works on the bridge over Spruce Street in downtown Olathe (oh-LAY-thuh) in July 1964 . . . *top right* . . . No. 3, the westbound Kansas City-Gallup, New Mexico mail train, passes by on the north track. The train was due out of Olathe at 9:44 a.m. and was scheduled into Gallup at 3:05 a.m. the following morning where it would combine with No. 7, the *Fast Mail Express*. *Bottom right* . . . A pair of GE U30CGs lead boxcars by mile 17 on January 12, 1985 near the old location of Zarah, Kansas. *Above: Mark Simonson; below and bottom right: Jim Primm; top right: Joe McMillan.*

Above . . . The main tracks have separate rights of way between Gardner and Edgerton, a distance of five miles. On a sunny spring morning in 1981, GP40X 3800 and SD39 4014 speed pass the Gardner station en route to Kansas City. *Below* . . . Five months later at the same spot, caboose 999240 tails westbound pigs while a GP39-2/GP20 duo curve into town with eastbound autoracks. The Gardner station building has since been removed. *Top right* . . . Late afternoon on May Day 1965 finds F7A 326 leading a classic A-B-B-B-B-B-A combination west out of Ottawa with a string of freight cars. SF30C 9533 (rebuilt GE U36C) rolls past the Ottawa station in September 1990 . . . *bottom right.* The line leading off to the left is the Tulsa Subdivision. In the background, a local sets out an ex-M-K-T Geep for the Midland Railway, a local excursion operator that purchased Santa Fe's 10.7-mile Baldwin District in May 1987. *Above: Jim Primm; below: Lance F. Garrels; top right: Joe McMillan; bottom right: David P. Oroszi.*

Above . . . Centropolis Road passes over the tracks at mile 57.8, just west of Ottawa. On September 26, 1976, a pair of GP39-2s and a U25B approach the bridge on the north main track with a westbound train of mixed freight. Condemned boxcars sit on the north pass awaiting their fate with the scrapper. *Below* . . . It was a rare occurrence when Santa Fe's rotary snowplow visited the Baldwin District in January 1979. The big plow had spent the previous week clearing the Pekin District in Illinois and made this side trip en route to western Kansas to open more branches. The Baldwin District (formerly the Lawrence District) is a remnant of the old Leavenworth, Lawrence and Galveston Railroad that built south from Lawrence through Ottawa to Coffeyville. The Lawrence-Baldwin segment was abandoned in 1964. *Above: Jim Primm; below: David A. Franz.*

For many years, the Santa Fe operated two pair of Kansas City-Tulsa passenger trains. *Above* . . . Train No. 211, *The Tulsan*, makes a station stop at Ottawa on May 1, 1965. The short train was due out of here at 5:55 p. m. and into Tulsa at 10:00 p. m. *Below* . . . At dawn on December 20, 1967, the camera catches both trains at Tulsa. On the right, No. 47, *The Oil Flyer*, has just arrived and on the left, No. 212, *The Tulsan*, prepares to depart. *The Oil Flyer* would be gone in three months, but Nos. 211 and 212 would last until the coming of Amtrak on May 1, 1971. The 198.9 mile Ottawa to Tulsa line was sold in 1990 in two segments. The Ottawa to Iola portion (52.6 miles) was sold to the KCT Railway Corporation (not to be confused with the Kansas City Terminal Railway of Kansas City) on May 3 and abandoned later that year. The rest of the line, along with the Moline and Coffeyville Subdivisions, became the South Kansas & Oklahoma Railroad on December 28th. *Above: Joe McMillan; below: Steve Patterson.*

Above . . . No. 212 makes a station stop at Bartlesville, Oklahoma, 50 miles north of Tulsa, on August 22, 1968 at 8:10 a. m. Twenty-one minutes later . . . *below* . . . the train stops for passengers at Caney, Kansas, on the Oklahoma-Kansas state line. GE U28CG 356 is on the point today. The four-car passenger train is due into Kansas City Union Station at 12:10 p.m., three hours and thirty-nine minutes from now. *Both photos: Joe McMillan.*

A pair of 800 class Alco RSD-15s speed west across Kansas Route 68 west of Ottawa at mile 63.8 on the Second District (now Emporia Subdivision) . . . *above*. It's December 8, 1968. Missouri Pacific's Osawatomie Subdivision (now UP's Hoisington Sub), Kansas City-Pueblo, Colorado, parallels the Santa Fe for a few miles through here. The MP track can be seen to the left of the 827. Santa Fe's main lines separate again between Melvern, mile 79.6, and Ridgeton, mile 87.6. *Below* . . . On May 12, 1987, SD45s 5361 and 5381 zip through Melvern westbound on the south main. The photo was taken from the Main Street overpass. The bridge in the photo carries 5th Street across the tracks. Melvern is a nice place to view trains. *Above: Joe McMillan; below: David P. Oroszi.*

A glance at the Santa Fe map would lead one to believe that at some point in the past the company purposely built the Ottawa Cutoff (as it was later called) between Holliday and NR Junction at Emporia as a shortcut west. The fact is, the line was pieced together over a period years. The first segment came with Santa Fe's purchase of the Leavenworth, Lawrence & Galveston in 1880—by then reorganized as the Kansas City, Lawrence and Southern Railroad. In addition to that railroad's main stem which ran south from Lawrence through Ottawa to Coffeyville, there was a branch running east from Ottawa to Olathe which had opened in August 1870. A fourteen mile connection linking Olathe with the Santa Fe main line at Holliday was built in 1882. This short line was built as the Kansas City and Olathe, a Santa Fe construction subsidiary. Two years later, another Santa Fe company, the Kansas City and Emporia Railroad, completed a 56 mile line between Ottawa and Emporia, completing the gap. The through line was upgraded and eventually became the Ottawa Cutoff and it remains today the principal route west of Kansas City. For years, the Cutoff was designated as the Second District of the Eastern Division. In the 1980s, it became successively the Second Subdivision, Ottawa Subdivision and finally, with the reorganization of August 15, 1990, the Emporia Subdivision of the Eastern Region.

Left . . . Bicentennial SD45-2 5700 negotiates the crossover from the south to the north main track at Ridgeton with the westbound *Super C*. The date is April 12, 1975. The fast Chicago to Los Angeles freighter will run another year before its discontinuance in May 1976. At nearly 9:00 p.m. five years later . . . *above* . . . GP40X 3807 leads westbound freight at the same location. *Left: Jim Primm; above: Lance F. Garrels and Mark Simonson.*

Santa Fe's station and tool house at Lebo, Kansas, 37 miles west of Ottawa, were decorated by the Eastern Division to honor the nation's 200th birthday. For several years the structure, shown in March 1976 . . . *above* . . . added color to an otherwise ordinary right of way. By late 1985, it had been restored to its yellow livery. The station was still standing in mid-1991, but it had been severely damaged in a storm and will probably be torn down. *Below* . . . On January 31, 1976, U23C 7505 leads a westbound by the bright building. *Above: Lee Berglund; below: Jim Primm.*

Emporia was headquarters for the Eastern Division for over a hundred years. In the early days, as many as a thousand employees worked here. Emporia was an important Santa Fe location until management began phasing out operations in the 1980s. Two important events sealed Emporia's fate. The first occurred on April 27, 1986 when the Eastern and Kansas City Divisions were consolidated with headquarters at Kansas City. The second event occurred in June 1990 when train crews began running through between Kansas City and Newton, Arkansas City and Wellington. Unfortunately, Emporia was too close to the major terminal at Kansas City to fit management's plans to lengthen crew districts. The engineer eases SD40-2 5037 on the point of westbound pigs . . . *above* . . . to a stop beside Emporia's impressive station and office building on October 27, 1977. The 5037 had been delivered new a few days prior, but tragically, the unit will be destroyed in five months in a terrible accident in California. *Below* . . . Two trains pause at Emporia for crew changes in February 1982: The 5182 heads train 803 (Los Angeles-Kansas City) and rotary plow 199361 trails the caboose of a special taking the machine west to stand by for a storm raging in New Mexico. *Above: David A. Franz; below: Mark Simonson.*

A large stone station and office building was built at Emporia in 1883 and 1884. Years later, in 1925 and 1926, a new building was built around the old one resulting in a very tasteful structure. William Allen White, famous editor of the *Emporia Gazette*, editorialized at the time, "This station is the best station on the Santa Fe railroad. It is not so elaborate as the station, offices, Harvey House and curio store at Albuquerque, but as a station it is the best Santa Fe station of all." *Top left* . . . Brand new B36-7 7491 stops on the north main at Emporia for a new crew. Santa Fe business car *Atchison* reflects the late evening lights on a November night in 1980. . . *above*. Emporia's roundhouse was one of the largest remaining on the system when photographed behind GE B23-7 6382 and mates on March 29, 1981 . . . *bottom left*. The facility has since been torn down. *Below* . . . SD40-2 5108 speeds west by long-abandoned Merrick tower at the west end of Emporia yard. There are three main tracks through here, from Wiggam, mile 107.1, east of Emporia to Ellinor, mile 124.5. The track curving away from the south main is the "electric lead" to the eastbound yard. (See also page 132.) *Top left: Mark Simonson; bottom left and above: Lance F. Garrels; below: David A. Franz.*

In April 1879, the Kansas City, Emporia & Southern built south from Emporia 64 miles to the Greenwood county line. From that point, the Elk & Chautauqua continued the line southward to Howard, reaching there on December 31st. In 1886, the remaining 8.1 miles were completed to Moline on the Chanute-Wellington line. The Howard District served its communities for over 90 years until abandoned on April 16, 1975. Local trains 97 and 98 (1281 and 1282 after January 1, 1971) operated on a down-one-day-and-back-the-next schedule for many years. Two years before abandoment . . . *above* . . . No. 1281 crosses the Cottonwood River outside Emporia behind GP7 2751. *Below* . . . CF7 2555 pilots a five car No. 1281 past the Olpe, Kansas station at mile 10.1 on February 2, 1974. *Two photos: David A. Franz.*

Strong City, Kansas, named for William Barstow Strong, president of the Santa Fe from 1881 to 1889, is located at mile 131.7, 19.6 miles west of Emporia on what is now the Newton Subdivision of the Eastern Region, but was for years the First District of the Middle Division. Most through freight traffic diverges at Ellinor, 7 miles east of Strong City, and continues southwest through Arkansas City and Wellington to Texas and California. We will follow the original main line and its connected branches west to Colorado, then return to Emporia on page 132 and follow the routes to Oklahoma and Texas.

The handsome brick station at Strong City was closed in April 1982, but still stands in 1991. *Above* . . . On September 3, 1988, train 304 (Kansas City-La Junta) rushes by the building behind SDF45 5981, SD45-2 booster 5510 and a GP20. Built in 1887, the old Bazar District linked Strong City with Bazar, a distance of 11.7 miles. The branch was later cut back to Cottonwood Falls, just across the river from Strong City. *Right* . . . In July 1979, three units off a local cross the Cottonwood River on the remnant of the Bazar District to switch a grain elevator. This short spur—used frequently for car storage—has since been removed. *Strong City station sign (1-23-82): Jim Primm; telephone in abandoned Strong City station (7-16-83): Joe McMillan; above: James Mitchell; right: David A. Franz.*

Neva (NEE-vah), 4.1 miles west of Strong City, is the junction with the 153.8 mile Strong City Subdivision, built in 1887 and 1888 to tap the rich farmlands of central Kansas. The branch remains a heavy-duty grain route today and can be very busy during the harvest season. In 1986, Santa Fe secured trackage rights over the Wichita Subdivision of the Oklahoma, Kansas & Texas Railroad (M-K-T) from Lost Springs (mile 25.5) south through Marion and Peabody to Wichita. (Before its demise, this was Rock Island's Kansas City-Herington-Texas main line. It now constitutes the Herington and McPherson Branches of Union Pacific's Wichita Division.) These trackage rights markedly improved service off the Strong City Sub by allowing Gulf Coast grain trains to run south to Wichita or Newton (via Peabody) and then down Santa Fe's Arkansas City Subdivision toward Texas. Prior to this arrangement, Texas grain trains were faced with a time consuming run around movement at Emporia. *Above . . .* Train LKK01, the Newton-Abilene turn, curves off the Strong City Sub onto UP's Herington Branch at Lost Springs on September 19, 1989. Later . . . *below* . . . the same train approaches Marion, Kansas on UP rails. At Peabody, the local will return to the Santa Fe for the final 16.8 miles to Newton. *Both photos: Mel Finzer.*

Above . . . In the 1970s and 1980s, local trains 1343 and 1344 served the north end of the Strong City District between Abilene and Superior, Nebraska. No. 1343 would go north on Monday, Wednesday and Friday and No. 1344 would return the following day. On September 3, 1983, the camera records No. 1344 rounding the curve at mile 138 south of Lovewell, Kansas behind B23-7s 6365, 6366, 6403 and 6355.

Technology caught up with Santa Fe depots in the early 1980s. New computer and communication systems enabled the railroad to achieve efficiencies by centralizing station activities into regional offices. Many Santa Fe stations had been closed earlier, of course, but in March 1981, the company began a concerted effort to close hundreds of stations across the system. By March 1985, over 300 agencies had been closed. Most of the doomed buldings were located in Kansas, Oklahoma and Texas, but virtually all of the railroad was affected. Many depots were razed, but many survive today as museums, city halls, summer cottages, offices and residences. The Bovina, Texas, Ashland and Carvel, Kansas, and Blair, Oklahoma stations became attractive homes. Sentinel, Okla. is a police station while Coats, Kansas is a veterinarian's office and Pawnee Rock is a service station. Tipton, Kansas became a club house at a golf course and Elmdale is a savings and loan office. Sadly, other buildings lie derelict on farms and ranches. *Right* . . . In better times, Aurora (named after Aurora, Illinois), 44 miles north of Abilene, was the site of this handsome building. Longford, mile 78.4, was named for an English colony near Dublin, Ireland. Its attractive white station was closed in January 1983 and removed shortly thereafter. *Above: David A. Franz; Aurora station (7-3-71): Lee Berglund; Longford station (5-9-76): Joe McMillan.*

Above . . . On a sunny day in August 1975, F9A 285C and three mates wheel grain south at Webber, Kansas, about five miles south of the Nebraska state line. Later . . . *top right* . . . the same train accelerates across Rock Island's Omaha to Denver/Colorado Springs line at Courtland, mile 133.7. A decade earlier, an observer might have been rewarded by the passing of No. 8, Rock Island's eastbound *Rocky Mountain Rocket*. It was due by here before 8:00 p.m. Westbound No. 7 would pass through after midnight. The Rock Island is long gone, but this portion of its route is still in place. The Kyle Railroad operates about 360 miles of the line, plus other branches in the area. Unit grain trains for the Gulf Coast are interchanged to the Santa Fe here. Five years later . . . *bottom right* . . . the Courtland depot has a new coat of paint. Local freight 1344 makes an air test after picking up some cars for Abilene. The date is March 1, 1980; the Rock Island will be history in just 30 days. The Courtland station was closed a year later and moved to a site nearby. *Above and top right: Jim Primm; bottom right: Lance F. Garrels.*

Top left . . . October 1, 1981 finds B23-7 6378 on a work train beside Santa Fe's Superior, Nebraska depot. For many years, Santa Fe had trackage rights over the Chicago and North Western from the Nebraska state line to Superior, a distance of about two miles, and joint use of the station and yard. The C&NW ceased operations over its Superior line (Seward-Superior) in 1972 because of a bridge washout. To protect its connections and interest, the Santa Fe purchased C&NW's Superior trackage, depot and yard on April 1, 1976.

The Minneapolis District branched off the Strong City District at Manchester, Kansas, mile 72.8. The 43.1 mile line, built in 1887 as the Minneapolis Extension, ran northwest to Barnard, named for a local Santa Fe manager. The line was abandoned on August 1, 1984. Bottom left . . . Four years prior to the line's closure, GP39-2 3703 idles at the point of the Abilene roadswitcher at Minneapolis, mile 24.1, while the crew has lunch. It's 108 degrees on July 1, 1980. Two years later, in September 1982 . . . above . . . two-car local No. 1351 behind GP39-2s 3692 and 3669 pauses on the Solomon River bridge at Minneapolis while the crew gets permission to cross UP's Solomon Branch. Right . . . CF7 2561 idles in front of the Abilene station, September 14, 1978. Two photos left page: Lance F. Garrels; two photos this page David A. Franz.

The 102.5 mile Salina Subdivision leaves the Strong City Sub at Abilene and wanders west and northwest through Salina and Lincoln to Osborne. The 80.8 mile Salina to Osborne segment was built as the Salina Northern in 1916 and acquired by the AT&SF in 1924 through a lease arrangement. Santa Fe trains have trackage rights over Union Pacific's Salina Subdivision (Kansas City-Denver main line) from West Abilene to East Salina, 19.9 miles. *Below . . .* B23-7 6357 leads local 1334 (Salina-Emporia) onto the UP main at East Salina, August 13, 1979. Years later, in May 1990 . . . *above . . .* GP39-2 3699 idles beside the Salina station. *Above: Tom Carlson; below: Lance F. Garrels.*

Below . . . Local LMI14 rumbles across the South Fork of the Solomon River at Osborne, Kansas on November 9, 1984. (On May 1, 1984, designations for Santa Fe's local trains changed from four-digit numbers to alpha-numeric symbols. The first letter indicates the train type, i.e., "L" for local, "R" for roadswitcher. The next two letters indicate the division; in this case, "MI" for Middle Division. [After the railroad was reorganized into six divisions on May 15, 1988, the division initials were changed to reflect the new division names.] The last two digits of the train designation are sequential numbers used to differentiate the various locals on the same division. On January 1, 1991, local train nomenclature was revised again: the second letter was changed to designate the region, i.e., "E" for Eastern, "C" for Central, and so on, and the third letter was modified to indicate the superintendent's territory, usually an "A," "B" or "C." Local train LMI14, for example, became the LKK14 in 1988 and the LEC14 in 1991.) *Above* . . . The Osborne-Abilene local is stopped at Lincoln, Kansas, mile 56.9, in December 1980 while the crew enjoys lunch nearby. *Below: David A. Franz; above: Lance F. Garrels.*

Abilene was home to former general and President of the United States, Dwight D. Eisenhower. To honor the centennial of his birth, the National Archives organized a series of events including the chartering of three trains on October 14, 1990 to transport World War II veterans from a reunion in Kansas City to Abilene. The Union Pacific, Burlington Northern—operating over the UP—and the Santa Fe each assembled trains for the occasion. The BN debuted its rebuilt EMD F-units, BN-1 and BN-2, while the UP featured its famous 4-8-4 844. After the passengers detrained at Abilene, all three trains proceeded west on the UP to Solomon where each was turned on the wye. *Left* . . . After turning, Santa Fe's train behind new GP60Ms 103 and 120 pulls through the north pass. Later . . . *above* . . . all three trains pose awaiting return to Abilene to load up for the journey back to Kansas City. *Below* . . . Late that afternoon, Santa Fe's seven-car special speeds between the elevators at Navarre, Kansas (mile 44.4) on the Strong City Sub en route to Kansas City. *Three photos: Joe McMillan.*

Santa Fe rails reached Newton, Kansas, 73 miles west of Emporia, in July 1871. Like Emporia, Newton was a division headquarters for years, but lost much of its prominence in the 1980s. This was home of the Middle Division and later, starting in May 1986, the Kansas Division. On August 15, 1990, however, the llinois Division and part of the Kansas Division merged to form the Eastern Region with headquarters at Kansas City. Unlike Emporia, Newton remains a crew change point, and several local freights still originate there. Its attractive passenger station was built in 1929 and 1930 and is used today by Amtrak to serve trains 3 and 4, the *Southwest Chief*. On April 8 and 9, 1986, the railroads of Kansas sponsored the Sunflower State Operation Lifesaver Special to promote grade crossing safety. The train, led by locomotives of the UP, KCS, SP, BN and M-K-T, was routed over the Santa Fe from Kansas City to Wichita (see page 218) via Topeka and Newton, then over the Missouri Pacific and Union Pacific north to Salina and back to Kansas City. The special is shown at Newton . . . *above* . . . during one of the safety presentations. *Below* . . . Years earlier, in August 1970, the nocturnal camera registers F7A 341 on Train No. 23, the former *Grand Canyon*, during a station stop at Newton. *Above: Joe McMillan; below: David K. Webb.*

Between 1879 and 1881, Santa Fe constructed a branch bypassing Newton to the north. The 98.5 mile McPherson District connected the main line at Florence, 28.2 miles east of Newton to what was then the main line at Ellinwood, 74.3 miles west of Newton. In 1970, the eastern ten miles of the branch between Florence and Marion was abandoned in favor of trackage rights over Rock Island's Herington-Ft. Worth main line (later OKT [M-K-T], now UP's Herington Branch) between Peabody and Marion. In March 1981, trackage rights were also obtained over MP's McPherson Subdivision—now UP's McPherson Branch—between Newton and McPherson, 29.2 miles. This route is now Santa Fe's primary connection to the McPherson Sub. A pair of local freights originate at McPherson, but their schedules and frequencies vary according to seasonal needs. There is also a scheduled turn from Newton to McPherson over the UP. *Below . . .* GP39-2 3609 idles at McPherson in April 1989. The east end of the station was removed several years ago giving the building a rather truncated appearance. The building at Conway, Kansas, photographed in October 1974 . . . *above . . .* was one of the most attractive structures on the branch until it was torn down in 1983. *Below: Mel Finzer; above: collection of Joe McMillan.*

Left . . . A Cessna-eye view catches local LKK34 (now LEC34) rounding the curves west of Little River, Kansas on October 9, 1990 en route to Lyons. Little River, home of the "Redskins," is located at mile 66.2, 19 miles west of McPherson. Collinwood Grain elevators dominate the small town, as they do in many Kansas towns. *Below* . . . Later, LKK34 enters Lyons, mile 78.1, to perform switching. Behind the train and barely discernible, is the crossing of UP's Hutchinson Branch (Wichita-Geneseo). Shortly, the engines will return to the crossing and travel south over the UP to switch the American Salt plant, a process that can take several hours. The plant is out of the photo at right. Note the "county seat" style brick depot in the lower left. The station was closed in March 1983, but still stands in 1991. *Redskins and Lyons signs: Joe McMillan; aerial views Mel and Vern Finzer.*

Above . . . Lyons was still an open agency when photographed in June 1981. Note the unusual positioning of the train order signal across the tracks from the station. GP38 3527 idles on the passing track with a short train from the Little River District. Santa Fe tracks crossed the old Frisco Burrton Subdivision (Wichita to Ellsworth) just west of the station. In 1972, Santa Fe secured trackage rights over this branch from the crossing north to Lorraine, Kansas (17.1 miles) to a connection with the Little River District. The 20.6 mile segment from Little River to Lorraine was abandoned in June 1972 when the Frisco trackage rights were obtained. After the Frisco became part of Burlington Northern on September 21, 1980, the Burrton Sub was abandoned between Buhler (40 miles northwest of Wichita) and Ellsworth, 61.7 miles. Because of the trackage rights agreement, however, BN still owns the orphaned section used by the Santa Fe between Lyons and Lorraine. *Below* . . . GP7s 2684 and 2713 head north out of Lyons on Frisco rails with a four car train for Galatia on July 5, 1973. Snow-filled cuts west of Holyrood in February 1979 . . . *top right* . . . exercise the rotary plow. *Bottom right* . . . When the Galatia station was photographed in September 1968, it was in need of a coat of paint, which it never got. The agency was closed shortly thereafter. *Above: Jim Primm; below: Lee Berglund; top right: John Arbuckle; bottom right: Howard Killam.*

Our return to the main line finds us in the cab of F40PHR 254 on Amtrak No. 3, the *Southwest Limited*, with Santa Fe engineer Orville Brunner racing west of Newton on the Second District, July 18, 1983. The train was scheduled out of Newton at 5:30 a.m. and into Dodge City at 7:45; 153.1 miles in 135 minutes, or an average of 68 m.p.h. with one intermediate station stop! In the eight years since these photos were taken, the train has been renamed the *Southwest Chief*, the territory has become the La Junta Subdivision, Amtrak train and engine crews have succeeded Santa Fe personnel and the average speed has increased to 70.1 m.p.h. *Both photos: Joe McMillan.*

Above . . . Train 304 pauses at Halstead, Kansas on April 2, 1990 awaiting clearance from a track gang ahead. Halstead is located at mile 194.6, 9.8 miles west of Newton. Santa Fe's only SF30B leads the westbound train. The 6419 (formerly 7200) was built from U23B 6332 at Cleburne shops in 1987 as a prototype for a proposed remanufacturing program for the 6300-6348 series U23Bs. Management decided to sell the U23Bs instead of rebuilding them, leaving the 6419 unique to the roster. [See also Volume 1, page 98.] The Santa Fe annually operates—usually in August—a shipper's special from Hutchinson to Garden City and return for the Kansas Grain and Feed Dealers Association. On August 31, 1989, after unloading its passengers, the special deadheads out of Hutchinson toward Topeka and Kansas City. *Above: Mel Finzer; below: Keel Middleton.*

Above . . . The 1989 annual Kansas Grain and Feed Dealer Association special speeds eastbound through Zenith, Kansas, mile 251.1, 32.8 miles west of Hutchinson. Motive power for the train varies from year to year, but today the 101-5260-100 (SDFP45/SDF40-2/SDFP45) do the honors. At Topeka, the 100 and some of the passenger cars will be dropped off for the Railroad Days celebration. (This is the same train pictured on page 17.)

The original main line west of Hutchinson was built in 1872 and followed the Arkansas River through Great Bend on what was for years the Fifth District of the Middle Division, now the Hutchinson Subdivision of the Eastern Region. Even today, the mileposts are numbered consecutively from Hutchinson to Dodge City via Great Bend. In 1886, the company built the "Hutchinson Extension" across the "Great Bend" from Hutchinson to Kinsley, cutting off 14.3 miles and providing a faster route west. Mileposts on the cutoff are numbered consecutively from Hutchinson to Kinsley where an engineering "equation" returns the sequencing to that of the original main line.

There are two highway overpasses at Sylvia, Kansas, one east of town and one west, offering the photographer a rare opportunity to record trains in western Kansas from an overhead perspective. U. S. Highway 50 crosses the main track west of town at mile 247.1. On April 2, 1990, train 304, photographed earlier at Halsted (page 65), curves through Sylvia enroute to Dodge City. East of town, the old Route 50 overpass (mile 245.9) is the vantage point to view the passing of train 344 (Kansas City-Denver) behind the 5381-8166-3806-5123 (SD45/C30-7/GP40X/SD40-2). It's 3:20 p. m., August 21, 1990. *Above: Mel Finzer; below: David P. Oroszi; left page: Jim Primm.*

Left . . . One hour and twenty-six minutes after passing through Sylvia, train 344 approaches the east end of Belpre (BEL-pree) siding at mile 284.1. Although some are replaced every year, semaphore signals are still prevalent in 1991 on the La Junta Subdivision, and further west into northeastern New Mexico. Below . . . B23-7 6383 leads a westbound into the north passing siding at Kinsley on June 21, 1981. Kinsley, mile 302.4, is the junction between the original main track, now the Hutchinson Subdivision, and the La Junta Sub. Note the roof-mounted station sign on the depot, an unusual feature for Santa Fe structures. Offerle, Kansas . . . above . . . lies at mile 324.7, eight miles west of Kinsley. Had you been standing beside the track one afternoon in June 1984, you might have seen this westbound rushing through town with horns blaring for the Walnut Street crossing. Offerle's station was closed in 1981 and has since been removed. Power for this piggyback freight is a trio of 4000 class SD39s. These locomotives were renumbered into the 1556-1575 series between October 1985 and February 1986. Most SD39s are now mated with slugs and assigned to yard duties at Barstow and Kansas City. EMD GP60s now occupy the 4000 series. Left: David P. Oroszi; above: David Lichtenberg; below: Jim Primm.

Santa Fe rails reached Dodge City in September 1872 and Dodge quickly became the most notorious of all the Kansas cattle towns. Other locations on the Union Pacific and Santa Fe had perhaps shared this distinction for a period of time, but Dodge was closest to the great cattle country of Texas and New Mexico and its notoriety lasted longest of any of them. Dodge City was a wild and rowdy place until law and order was finally established by famous lawmen such as Wyatt Earp and Bat Masterson. Over 400,000 Texas longhorns had been shipped east from Dodge by 1882. The town lost some of its prominence as railroads built west and into Texas and Oklahoma, but it is still at the center of a large grain producing area and it continues to be an important cattle town.

Certainly the most striking structure in Dodge City today is the old Santa Fe station, office building and former El Vaquero Harvey House hotel. The building was built in 1897 and was for years the headquarters of the Western Division, which was absorbed by the Middle Division on September 1, 1958. Most of the huge building is currently vacant, however, Amtrak still uses the ticket office and waiting room to serve its customers. Santa Fe employees were relocated to a small building nearby in May 1991. *Top left*... The Dodge City station is viewed from the southeast on April 4, 1990 as the Dodge switcher (GP7-slug set) idles in the yard. *Above*... The west end of the station in August 1990. The street at the left of the building is Wyatt Earp Blvd. *Bottom left*... Located in a small park east of the station are two huge sun dials. The dials were constructed by a Santa Fe division engineer in 1897 and further refined in 1928. They have been an attraction to the traveling public for over 90 years. The official time zone change is at the Finney-Kearny county line at mile 415.3, 62.8 miles west of Dodge. For operating purposes, however, Dodge City has always been the time change location for rail crews. For that reason, one sun dial displays Central Standard Time while the other depicts Mountain Standard Time. This photograph was taken on June 24, 1990. *Top left: Mel Finzer; bottom left: Joe McMillan; above: David P. Oroszi.*

Great Bend is appropriately located on the "great bend" of the Arkansas River on what is now the Hutchinson Subdivision. Santa Fe's original main line reached here on July 30, 1872. After the Hutchinson-Kinsley cutoff was built in 1886, the line became a branch, and it remains so today. Local passenger trains 311 and 312 served the Great Bend line until they were discontinued on June 13, 1965. Santa Fe's two Budd RDC cars were assigned to these trains for several years. *Bottom . . .* Great Bend's fine white brick station, photographed in January 1971, has changed little since its completion in 1911. *Below . . .* Merger red GP35 2814 leads Hutchinson Sub local LKK34 by the station on September 20, 1989. Note that the train order signal and several yard tracks have been removed during the intervening 18 years.

The 120 mile Great Bend Subdivision (Great Bend-Scott City) joins the Hutchinson Sub west of the depot. *Above* . . . During a March 1978 snow storm, the Great Bend local got caught at Scott City without a plow. The snow packed nose of GP7 2052 is evidence of the difficult all night return to Great Bend, where the units are shown the next morning. *Below* . . . GEs 7509 and 7909 (U23C/U28CG) move an eastbound under the old coal tower at Great Bend on December 19, 1978. The tower still stands in 1991, but the units are gone. *Great Bend sign: Joe McMillan; middle left: Mel Finzer; bottom left, above and below: Lee Berglund.*

The Great Bend Subdivision was built in 1886 and 1887, a period of great Santa Fe expansion into the Plains. For years, the branch was served by local freights 69 and 70, but by the late 1980s, the trains had been redesignated LKK38 (eastbound) and LKK39 (westbound). The local operated to Scott City twice a week, alternating with the Jetmore train (Great Bend-Larned-Jetmore). *Above* . . . LKK39 accelerates westward out of Ness City, Kansas on October 23, 1990 behind GP38 2308 and GP35 2837. *Below* . . . GP35s 2814 and 2887 wheel eastbound LKK38 between Alamota and Beeler, Kansas on October 7, 1989. Commercially grown sunflowers dominate the foreground. Heavy snow in January and February 1979 crippled the Great Bend District. A push plow, used in January to open the line, was wrecked and destroyed in a derailment, along with one of the GP7s pushing it. Rotary plow 199361 was called to help out and is shown westbound on February 3rd . . . *bottom right* . . . at a rural road crossing near Timken, about 20 miles west of Great Bend. Heavier drifts west of Dighton were tackled the next day. *Top right* . . . After the line was opened, GP38 3555, GP20 3153 and the rotary pass the Ness City station returning to Great Bend, February 4, 1979. The Ness City station, incidentally, still stands in 1991. *Above and below: Tom Carlson; top right: Jim Primm; bottom right: Lee Berglund.*

Top left . . . A section gang trackman watches a ten-car LKK39 pass through Nekoma, 39 miles west of Great Bend on September 27, 1989. Seven years earlier . . . *bottom left* . . . B23-7 6392 passes its caboose, or waycar in Santa Fe parlance, while switching at Nekoma. Though cabooses were common until 1989 and 1990, many Santa Fe locals now operate without them. By mid-1991, there were less than a hundred caboose cars on the roster, down from nearly 670 cars in 1985. Most of the waycars in service today are the newer International Car center-cupola cabooses built in 1978 and 1981. There were less than ten cars remaining of the design illustrated by class Ce-1 car 999282. *Above* . . . On October 10, 1990, LKK39 moves eastbound out of Bazine, mile 52.5, behind a pair of GP39-2s: 3406 and 3677. The grain elevators on the horizon above the engines are at Ness City, mile 64.1, and Laird, mile 72.5. *Top left: Mel Finzer; bottom left: Lee Berglund; above: Mel and Vern Finzer.*

We return to the Fifth District (Hutchinson Subdivision) and witness Missouri Pacific GP7 1680 and two cars eastbound near Nickerson, Kansas on May 7, 1974 . . . *top left*. Trains operating over UP's Hutchinson Branch (ex-MP Hutchinson Sub), Wichita to Geneseo, had trackage rights over the Santa Fe from YA Junction, just outside Hutchinson, to ST Junction at Sterling, a distance of 12.9 miles. (In April 1991, this line and others were leased to the Chicago West Pullman Corporation for operation as the Kansas Southwestern Railroad.) The same day . . . *middle left* . . . CF7 2611 switches the Great Bend Industrial Spur at Great Bend. This two-mile line leaves the Hutchinson Sub main line at mile 274.6, five miles west of Great Bend, and serves several customers, including Fuller Brush. *Bottom left* . . . F7As 238L and 229L scoot along the Fifth District with a plow near Dundee, eight miles west of Great Bend on February 25, 1971. The train is en route to the Larned District (Larned-Jetmore). *Above* . . . F3A 19 leads a pair of freight F7Bs across Ash Creek west of Pawnee Rock on April 23, 1971 with a train of mixed freight for Dodge City. *Below* . . . During the early 1970s, Santa Fe operated a Dodge City to Emporia train routed via the Fifth District on Sundays. On September 12, 1971, a consist which would be more at home on a passenger train leads eastbound freight at Pawnee Rock. *Five photos: Lee Berglund.*

Larned, Kansas, located at mile 291.8 on the Hutchinson Subdivision, 22.3 miles southwest of Great Bend, is the junction point with the 46.2 mile Jetmore Sub. Larned's brick station, built in 1905, was closed in November 1982 and converted to a restaurant. *Bottom right . . .* The Jetmore local idles at the Larned station prior to heading out on the branch, May 14, 1974. *Top right . . .* CF7 2571 and GP7 2729 shove a hopper into the Pawnee County Co-op at Larned in July 1977. *Above . . .* Garfield, Kansas, named for president James A. Garfield, is located on the Hutchinson Sub, 10.7 miles southwest of Larned. During the wheat harvest on a hot Independence Day 1982, B23-7 6370 and mates switch the Garfield Co-op elevators. The harvest doesn't take a holiday! Garfield is normally served by a side trip of the Great Bend-Jetmore local. The depot closed in April 1982 and was torn down in September 1983. *Three photos: Lee Berglund.*

Santa Fe rails reached Jetmore, Kansas, at the end of the 46.2 mile Larned Subdivision, on August 25, 1887. Like all branches in the area, the line is subject to heavy drifting during winter storms. *Above* . . . On February 5, 1983, five units push a plow east of Burdett. This is probably the last time a wedge plow was used on the Santa Fe. All remaining push plows were scrapped shortly thereafter, including this one. The company now relies on locomotives with plow pilots to keep the lines clear, and the rotary if that fails. Four years later, on March 31, 1987 . . . *below* . . . the rotary eats through a small drift west of Burdett. The spring sun has already melted most of the accumulation. *Two photos this page: Lee Berglund.*

Above . . . Mr. Herb Bach was agent at Jetmore when this photo was taken in May 1976. Although the telephone was the principal means of communication, the telegraph was still functional at the time and was used infrequently as a back up, or merely to keep one's skills tuned. Note the ubiquitous Remington typewriter, gooseneck telephone, train order box (behind the telegraph sounder) and timetable (in the window at left); in all, an ageless scene dispatched to oblivion by modern technology. *Below* . . . The Jetmore station was photographed in February 1982, nine months before it was closed, moved to a site south of town and converted to a residence. *Above: Joe McMillan; below: Jim Primm.*

Back to Dodge, partner. *Above* . . . The early morning summer sun falls on the east end of the Dodge City station in June 1990 while GP7 1327 (and slug) idles in the yard. *Below* . . . In October 1980, GE B23-7 6402 sticks its nose out of the Dodge City roundhouse—since torn down. In the early days of this century, there were nearly a hundred Santa Fe engine houses. Today they are almost extinct. While a few Santa Fe roundhouses still exist in 1991, none are used to maintain locomotives. (The former Santa Fe Redondo Junction roundhouse in Los Angeles is a notable exception, but it is now owned and operated by Amtrak.) Amarillo, Texas had the last active Santa Fe roundhouse prior to its demolition in April 1990. *Above: Joe McMillan; below: Mark Simonson.*

Before 1908, Santa Fe's only route to the West Coast was over Raton and Glorieta Passes in northeastern New Mexico. Steep grades and other operational problems encouraged early builders to find a better route. One bypass studied by the company that would have alleviated the situation was the Colmor Cutoff. This line would have left the main line at Dodge City and angled southwestward through Elkhart, Kansas, Boise City, Oklahoma to a connection with the Colorado and Southern at Clayton, New Mexico. Trackage rights would take trains to Mt. Dora, New Mexico, where they would return to Santa Fe rails through Farley to a connection with the main line at Colmor, 192 miles northeast of Albuquerque on what is now the Las Vegas Subdivision of the Central Region. The Dodge City and Cimarron Valley was incorporated to build this line and by July 1, 1913, its rails had reached Elkhart, Kansas. Enthusiasm for the route waned, however, and nothing else was done until the Elkhart & Santa Fe was incorporated in 1925 to continue the line west. By December 1st of that year, the tracks had been laid through Boise City to Felt, Oklahoma, and by November 1931, the line had been extended 36 miles beyond the C&S connection at Mt. Dora to Farley where construction stopped. Several factors teamed up to halt the project. First, the Belen Cutoff from the Texas-New Mexico border to the main line at Belen had been completed and was serving its intended purpose as an alternate route west with better grades than the original main line. Second, the railroad was caught up in the Depression and was experiencing a severe decline in traffic. The wheat crops blew away with harsh dust storms and, in general, the cutoff gave scant promise of profitability. In 1942, the line west of Boise City was abandoned and its rails ripped up for the war effort. Today, 159.2 miles of the old Colmor Cutoff remain as the C.V. (Cimarron Valley) Subdivision.

Above . . . On September 16, 1983, local 1515, the Dodge City-Satanta turn, leaves Dodge with 66 empty grain hoppers, a tank of fertilizer and waycar 999172. On the point are GP39-2s 3674 and 3675. It's 6:40 p.m. as the train crosses the Arkansas River on Cotton Belt rails. Santa Fe had trackage rights over the river on the Rock Island (later SSW) between CRIP Junction and CV Junction, 0.9 mile. Rock Island's Subdivision 21A connected Dodge City to the Kansas City-Tucumcari main line at Bucklin, Kansas, 26.5 miles. The line became the Dodge City Branch of the SSW when the Southern Pacific purchased the Tucumcari line in 1980. The branch was subsequently sold to the Dodge City, Ford and Bucklin Railroad, a short line which uses a former Santa Fe CF7 as power. *Above: David K. Webb.*

Many Santa Fe branch lines were served by mixed trains and the C. V. District was no exception. Mixed trains 173 and 174 ran between Dodge City and Boise City, departing Dodge on Monday, Wednesday and Friday, returning the next day. Mixed train service lasted until the coming of Amtrak, but the combination cars came off in mid-1969. *Middle left* . . . Train 174 pauses at Satanta for some switching on a hot August 15, 1968. GP7 2848 and F7B 268A are on the point and combination car 2544 brings up the markers. From the rear of No. 174 departing Satanta . . . *bottom left* . . . the camera catches mixed No. 185 stopping at the station. Combine 2640 trails the westbound train today. Trains 185 and 186 served the Manter District (Satanta-Pritchett, Colorado, 109.6 miles) on a tri-weekly schedule leaving Dodge on Sunday, Tuesday and Thursday. Later that afternoon . . . *below* . . . No. 174 stops at Montezuma, Kansas for switching. The conductor walks to the depot while the motors back through the house track. The founder of the town, familiar with the story of the Spanish conquest of Mexico, named the town Montezuma for the Aztec emperor and named the streets for historical figures associated with the conquest. Unfortunately, the station is gone; its location now marked by a sign. Combination car 2544, however, is preserved at the Illinois Railway Museum at Union, Illinois northwest of Chicago. *Five photos: Joe McMillan.*

Boise City, Oklahoma, named for Boise, Idaho, (although the "Boise" rhymes with "voice") is the county seat of Cimarron County, the westernmost county of the state, and incidentally, the only county in the nation to border four states (five, if you include Oklahoma): Kansas, Colorado, New Mexico and Texas. Boise City is only 35 miles from Kansas, 18 miles from Colorado, 27 miles from New Mexico and 15 miles from Texas! Santa Fe rails came relatively late to Boise City. As stated earlier, the Colmor Cutoff built through there in 1925, but this line was later cut back to Boise City. As early as 1893, Santa Fe sought to better its competitive posture between Denver and Galveston by building a line connecting Amarillo with the Colorado main line. Nothing was done, however, until 1930 when the railroad received permission to build from Amarillo through Boise City to Las Animas, Colorado, 21 miles east of La Junta. The line would shorten Santa Fe's Colorado-Texas route by 400 miles. Track was built north from Amarillo, reaching Boise City in mid-1931, but the infamous Dust Bowl and the Depression delayed the completion of the Boise City-Las Animas segment until February 1937. The Amarillo-Las Animas line is now the Boise City Subdivision of the Central Region.

Left . . . It's late in the afternoon of August 14, 1968. Mixed train No. 173 has just arrived at Boise City from Dodge City and the agent and brakeman are unloading express. After the train is turned, the crew will tie up for the night. Train 38 from La Junta has just also just arrived, so the Boise City yard will be busy for a few minutes. Above . . . Early the next morning, No. 174 pauses at Keyes, Oklahoma, 15.6 miles east of Boise City. A helium plant built here by the U. S. Bureau of Mines in 1959 was a source of revenue for Santa Fe until it closed in 1982. The second car in the train is an empty MHAX helium car returning to the plant. (About the only carload helium business on the Santa Fe today comes from a large plant at Exell, Texas on the Boise City Sub, 37 miles north of Amarillo.) Incidentally, it is only a myth that a loaded helium car is lighter than an empty one! Until it was abandoned in 1973, Keyes was also the western terminus of the 105 mile Beaver, Meade and Englewood Railroad, an affiliate of the M-K-T. *Both photos: Joe McMillan.*

Top left . . . A three-car No. 174 awaits an early morning departure from Boise City in August 1968. *Bottom left* . . . Storm clouds part for a few minutes on a cold windy day in February 1964 permitting the sun to briefly illuminate the station. From a perch high atop the Boise City Farmers Co-op elevator on April 3, 1990 . . . *above* . . . the camera records local LKC74 (now LEC74) pulling out of the yard for Dodge City. The line in the distance curving around the tall grain elevator is the main line to Las Animas. The Dodge City main (C. V. Subdivision) branches off the Boise City Sub at a wye just behind the photographer. The yard lead running off the photo at left led to a roundhouse, a portion of which still stands. Note the station in the center of the photo and the cluster of old frame elevators behind it. *Two photos left page: Joe McMillan; above: Mel Finzer.*

The 109.2 mile Manter Subdivision, built between 1923 and 1927, runs from Satanta, Kansas on the C. V. Sub to Pritchett, Colorado. *Top left* . . . On April 3, 1990, local LKC75 passes through Johnson City, Kansas, 46 miles northwest of Satanta, and later . . . *bottom left* . . . the eight car train leaves Manter. The setting sun . . . *above* . . . finds the local west of Walsh, Colorado near Vilas en route to a tie up at Springfield, about 15 miles away. *Three photos: Mel Finzer.*

Now, let's return to the La Junta Subdivision and continue west.

There are only a few interesting photo locations west of Dodge City on the La Junta Subdivision. Certainly one of the best spots is a pair of curves west of Howell, Kansas between miles 363 and 364 along U. S. Highway 50. *Above* . . . In August 1988, members of the Kansas Grain and Feed Dealers Association head back to Hutchinson from Garden City behind new GE DASH 8-40B 7410, the class unit. (The grain elevators on the horizon are at Cimarron, Kansas, 7 miles away.) Earlier that morning . . . *top right* . . . the seven car special prepares to leave Garden City. The 37.8 mile Garden City District left the main line just west of the station and ran north to Scott City where it crossed Missouri Pacific's Kansas City-Pueblo line (now UP's Hoisington Subdivision) and joined Santa Fe's Great Bend District. The MP crossing was removed in 1979, and the segment between Garden City and Shallow Water (30 miles) was sold on September 6, 1989 to the Garden City Northern, an affiliate of the Garden City Western Railway. Santa Fe retains the orphaned line between Shallow Water and Scott City, but it is not operated. From Garden City, the main line leads west through Coolidge, Kansas . . . *bottom right* . . . on the Kansas-Colorado border where we see U36C 8516 leading mixed freight west on May 14, 1980. Note the cantilever-mounted semaphore. *Above and top right: John Arbuckle; bottom right: Bruce D. Barrett.*

Above . . . The first station in Colorado is Holly, named for the Holly Sugar Company which developed much of the area. Its attractive depot was completed in 1912 and still stands in 1991. In 1906, the Holly Sugar Company and the American Beet Sugar Company organized two railroads to build lines on the north side of the Arkansas River to connect with the Santa Fe between Holly and Rocky Ford, Colorado. The Santa Fe took over the lines in March 1907 and joined them, forming the 93.5 mile Second District (later the A. V. District) of the Colorado Division. The beet line was abandoned in segments beginning in the early 1970s. The last remnants were sold to the KCT Railway Corporation on May 2, 1990. *Below* . . . McClave, located on the A. V. District at mile 43.6, was photographed on May 22, 1973, eight years before it closed. *Above: Jim Primm; below: collection of Joe McMillan.*

Lamar, Colorado . . . *above* . . . is located on the main line 27 miles west of Holly. On September 11, 1971, GP38 3555 (now 2355) passes the station with freight for the west. *Below* . . . On October 21, 1986, under dark skies, a short "Q train" passes through Las Animas en route to La Junta. This train was part of the Quality Service Network (QSN) series of short fast freights established in the fall of 1986 to connect selected key cities. The trains, designed to divert highway traffic to the rails, generally ran with two person crews over extended crew districts. La Junta was the major QSN hub. Six trains daily (three in the morning and three in the afternoon) arrived there, were quickly switched and sent on their way. While there are many "Q symboled" trains operating today, the QSN as it was originally established was phased out over the succeeding years. The last QSN trains to LaJunta and Denver operated in 1990 . *Above: Lee Berglund; below: Robert R. Harmen.*

Until May 15, 1988, La Junta was headquarters of the Colorado Division. Its main lines stretched west from Dodge City through La Junta to Denver, and from La Junta southwest to Albuquerque. The May 1988 consolidation divided the Colorado Division between the Kansas and New Mexico Divisions, and the August 1990 reorganization further juggled the lines between the new Eastern and Central Regions. The division office building, which is still used by the company, is located at 402 Santa Fe, some distance from the tracks. The La Junta passenger station, located at First and Colorado, was built in 1955 replacing a gigantic depot and Harvey House erected in 1895.

La Junta was another good place to view passenger trains. *Top left* . . . On January 25, 1970, the combined *Super Chief/El Capitan* pauses at La Junta during a regular station stop. Connecting with Santa Fe's premier passenger trains at La Junta were Denver trains 191/190 and 200/201. (The trains changed timetable directions at Pueblo, hence the double numbers.) E8m's 81 and 84 were assigned to these trains until their retirement in 1970. *Bottom left* . . . Both Denver trains sit side by side at La Junta on August 13, 1968. No. 190, at right, has just arrived and at 8:30 p. m., E8m 84 will ease No. 201 out of town for the four hour trip to Denver. *Below* . . . E8m 81 idles in the afternoon sun on the previous day. It will lead No. 201 that evening. *Above* . . . United Aircraft's Turbo Train refuels at La Junta on May 23, 1971 prior to heading east. The demonstrator had been on display at Baxter, Colorado (about eight miles southeast of Pueblo) during the inauguration of the Department of Transportation Test Center near Pueblo. *Top left: Ernie Robart; bottom left and above: Joe McMillan; below: Robert R. Harmen.*

Before heading up the Denver line, let's take a ride south on the Boise City District (now Boise City Sub), which leaves the La Junta Subdivision at Las Animas Junction, 21.3 miles east of La Junta. *Above* . . . An August 1968 thunderstorm drenches the Arkansas River Valley as we glance back from the cupola of caboose 999020 on train No. 38 (La Junta-Boise City) at mile 231, four miles south of Las Animas Junction on the Boise City District. The track was completely rebuilt with 112-pound welded rail ten years later to accommodate coal trains. *Below* . . . Later that day, the train stops at Springfield, Colorado (mile 173.1) to switch a grain elevator. Nos. 37 and 38 were still mixed trains when these photos were taken. Passengers were carried in the caboose and express in the old reefer ahead of it. *Above and below: Joe McMillan.*

Above . . . The switching having been completed, No. 38 passes South Junction leaving Springfield. Up front today is a matched A-B-B-B-A set of passenger F-units led by F3A 25. The track at the left is the west leg of the wye connecting the Manter District to the Boise City District. Trains operating on the Manter line share Boise City District trackage from here through Springfield to North Junction, where the 12.4 mile line to Pritchett diverges. *Right* . . . Springfield station in February 1982. *Above: Joe McMillan; right: Jim Primm.*

Above . . . Our return to La Junta finds us atop the Colorado Highway 109 overpass at the east end of the yard on November 21, 1987 as train 364 (Kansas City-Denver) eases into town on the north main behind the 3062 and 2819 (GP20/GP35). The brakeman is walking ahead to line the crossover switch to route the train into the yard. That's the Arkansas River in the distant center of the photograph.

Leaving La Junta, Pueblo Subdivision rails lead northwest through Rocky Ford (mile 565.6), Manzanola (mile 574.5) and Fowler (mile 583.1). Brick stations still stand at all three locations. At NA Junction, 8.5 miles west of Fowler, UP's Hoisington Subdivision (Kansas City-Pueblo) swings in from the east. The Santa Fe and Missouri Pacific had separate rights of way to Pueblo until August 1969 when a joint trackage agreement was implemented using portions of both railroads. The AT&SF and UP operate over the ex-MP main from NA Junction to mile 605.3, just west of Avondale, and over the Santa Fe from there to Pueblo Junction. The Denver & Rio Grande Western has trackage rights over the UP between Pueblo and Kansas City, making this 26 mile line a busy one. *Top right* . . . Bicentennial SD45-2s 5700 and 5701 power an officers special at Avondale on May 31, 1975. The train has just come from the DOT Test Center and has stopped on the east leg of the wye before returning east. The yard track in the foreground is the former Santa Fe main line through Avondale. The joint AT&SF-MP main is at the far left. *Bottom right* . . . A highway overpass at the west end of Avondale provides a nice vantage point. If you were there on August 13, 1977, you would have seen 4018-8515-7905 (SD39/U33C/U28CG) leading train 471, an eastbound NORX coal train, making the transition from the Santa Fe right of way to the Missouri Pacific. The front portion is on the MP while the rear (at the curve in the background) is on the AT&SF. The Santa Fe main line used to lie on the embankment at right. The track to the right of the engines is the west end of the siding. *Above: John Rus; two photos right page: Robert R. Harmen.*

Above . . . When photographed in January 1966, La Junta-Denver passenger train No. 201 was due into Pueblo at 2:25 p. m. and out at 3:15. (Between January 1959 and the mid-1960s, the Santa Fe passenger trains were physically combined with C&S Nos. 27 and 28 [Dallas-Denver] north of Pueblo.) *Below* . . . A trio of GP7s on the "Hill Drag" guide a string of empty ore hoppers by Pueblo Union Depot in May 1970. The switcher interchanged traffic between Pueblo Yard and the Colorado & Wyoming Railroad (serving the CF&I steel mill) on the Minnequa District southeast of town.

Above . . . Pueblo Yard, located north of downtown, was a joint AT&SF-C&S facility. It still serves Santa Fe and BN, but its importance diminished greatly during the 1980s. When this photo was taken in August 1977, however, it was still a busy place. D&RGW coal train 756 pulls down the main line behind three Rio Grande motors with 51 cars of coal for Gary, Indiana . The "B unit" at lower right is a RCE (Remote Control Equipment) car used to house air and radio equipment in remote helper operations. The equipment was later placed aboard locomotives, sending the RCE cars to scrap by early 1983. The D&RGW yard is left of the coal train. *Below* . . . Two years later, the camera records another view of the yard, this one slightly to the right of the one above. A 61-car coal train behind the 8076-6310-3657 (C30-7/U23B/GP39-2) slips out of the yard beside idling AT&SF and BN engines. Several tracks shown in these two photos have since been removed, including the one under the RCE car. *Top left: Steve Patterson; three other photos: Robert R. Harmen.*

Above . . . F9A 286L leads a westbound freight into Pueblo on April 1, 1973. Santa Fe rostered 36 F9s: 18 cab units (281L,C to 289L,C) and 18 boosters (281A,B to 289A,B). The entire class was gone by the fall of 1980; most of the cab units were converted to CF7s while the boosters went to scrap. Between November 1972 and January 1974, six of the cab units received yellow warbonnet noses, as illustrated by the 286L. This photo was taken from the Main Street overpass. Pueblo Union Depot is about two blocks behind the photographer. *Top right* . . . The 4.5 mile joint BN-AT&SF Minnequa Subdivision leaves the Santa Fe main line at Pueblo Junction and runs to Southern Junction where it connects with the joint D&RGW-BN line to Trinidad. All BN coal trains to and from Texas use the Minnequa Sub. On the Fourth of July 1986, the Hill Drag crosses Salt Creek at mile 121.1 on the Minnequa Sub behind ex-TP&W GP38 2374 and a GP20. The huge Colorado Fuel and Iron (CF&I) steel mill dominates the background. *Bottom right* . . . As stated earlier, the Missouri Pacific (now UP) and the Santa Fe share the main line between Pueblo Junction and NA Junction. In August 1976, MP 3064-3066-3099 (SD40/SD40/SD40-2) lead eastbound coal though the deep cut east of Pueblo Junction on jointly operated AT&SF track. *Three photos: Robert R. Harmen.*

The 39.7 mile Canon City Subdivision is a remnant of Santa Fe's attempt to build west through the Royal Gorge in 1878, an effort which led to armed conflict between Santa Fe and Denver & Rio Grande construction forces. The Rio Grande was also attempting to extend west, but there was room in the Gorge for only one track. The antagonists fired rifles at one another and sabotaged each others construction camps, but their dispute was finally resolved by the courts in Rio Grande's favor in 1879. Earlier in 1878, Santa Fe had won possession of Raton Pass in another confrontation with the Rio Grande. One can only speculate how history might have been changed if the Rio Grande had beaten Santa Fe to Raton Pass and the Santa Fe had built through the Royal Gorge.

In 1880, after the Royal Gorge issue had been settled, the Santa Fe sought to protect its coal business by building its own track to coal deposits west of Pueblo. The line was extended to Canon City in 1887, but much of the track between Pueblo and Portland (25 miles) was destroyed in a 1921 flood. The Santa Fe subsequently negotiated trackage rights over the D&RGW between the two points and dismantled its own line. In 1947, trackage rights were extended to Canon City, allowing Santa Fe to abandon the rest of the branch. The only AT&SF-owned trackage remaining today are some industry tracks along the line and a small yard at Canon City. Santa Fe still serves several customers on the Subdivision and occasionally hauls coal out of Clelland, eight miles east of Canon City.

Above . . . Colorado Division local trains 29 and 30 served the Canon City District daily except Sunday in the 1960s and RSD-5s were regular power. On May 3, 1967, Alco RSD-5 2137 idles at the point of No. 29 in front of the Rio Grande station at Canon City. Most of the 2100s disappeared from the roster between 1965 and 1970, but a few hung on until 1972. The 2137 was sold to EMD in 1968 for credit on new F45s. *Top right* . . . Sixteen years later, second generation EMDs have replaced RSD-5s on the local. Units 3650-3524 (GP39-2/GP38) switch hoppers in Santa Fe's small yard near the Canon City station. *Bottom right* . . . On January 6, 1990, GP30 2709 pulls a string of empty BN hoppers of out the Ideal Cement Plant at Portland. *Above: Steve Patterson; two photos right page: Bryan Bechtold.*

The paired D&RGW-AT&SF line between Pueblo and Denver, known as the Joint Line, has an interesting history. It started in 1872 when the Rio Grande completed a narrow gauge line from Denver to Pueblo. In 1882, Santa Fe gained entry to Denver by adding a third rail to the D&RG track, standard gauging the line. In the meantime, the Denver and New Orleans (a predecessor of the Colorado & Southern) built its line between the two cities along a route somewhat east of the Rio Grande. Frustrated by operating problems associated with the joint D&RG arrangement, Santa Fe constructed is own track north from Pueblo alongside the D&RG, reaching Denver in September 1887. In 1898, the Colorado & Southern was organized and purchased the D&NO line. A year later, the C&S reached agreements to use the Santa Fe between Pueblo and Bragdon, 11 miles, the D&RG (by then standard-gauged) from there to South Denver and the Santa Fe again from South Denver to Denver, 3.5 miles. (The AT&SF later obtained trackage rights over the C&S from South Denver to Denver.) A further agreement in 1915 allowed the C&S to abandon most of its Pueblo-Denver line. Three years later, on October 18, 1918, the Santa Fe and Rio Grande combined their two lines in a paired track arrangement and, as a Santa Fe tenant, granted C&S access to the joint facility. This arrangement remains in place today.

The visitor to today's Joint Line will be treated to a variety of trains, most of which are powered by BN and D&RGW locomotives. In 1991, the Santa Fe was operating only one regular train each way daily (symbols 344 and 443). Santa Fe crews keep busy, however. In addition to AT&SF trains, they also operate all Burlington Northern trains between Denver and Pueblo. BN, in turn, does Santa Fe's terminal and switching work in Denver. *Above . . .* The Santa Fe and Rio Grande lines pass separately through Pueblo, joining at Bragdon, 11 miles north of the city. On August 25, 1990, a pair of BN SD40-2s wait in the sunflowers at Bragdon behind a red block before proceeding north with BN pig train 091 (Houston-Seattle). *Top left . . .* A string of Burlington Northern U30Cs guide a southbound loaded coal train around the big curve at Santa Fe mile 628 south of Bragdon on May 30, 1974. Interstate 25 and the D&RGW track lie along the line of trees in the distant background. *Bottom left . . .* Denver-Kansas City train 443 speeds south through Fountain, Colorado, behind a set of four-motor units. *Above: Steve Patterson; top left: Robert R. Harmen; bottom left: Chuck Conway.*

111

Colorado Springs is the largest intermediate city on the Joint Line. Prior to 1975, the Rio Grande and the Santa Fe maintained separate rights of way through the city, with northbound trains of both railroads using the Santa Fe, and southbound trains the D&RGW. Under pressure from city fathers, the Santa Fe line was abandoned through Colorado Springs from Crews, 10 miles south of the city, to Palmer Lake, 23 miles north, in 1974 and 1975. The abandonment forced all trains onto the Rio Grande, which at the time was a satisfactory arrangement. Shortly thereafter, however, BN coal traffic on the Joint Line increased dramatically, creating a bottleneck. *Above* . . . Santa Fe's southbound Denver-La Junta passenger train stopped at Colorado Springs' joint Rio Grande-Rock Island station, while the northbound train served the Santa Fe station. No. 191, behind E8m 84, stops at the D&RGW-CRI&P station on August 9, 1968, while . . . *top right* . . . No. 200 unloads passengers, baggage and mail at the Santa Fe station a year earlier. (Note the 625 class Baldwin switcher at left.) *Bottom right* . . . During its last year of operation (after the retirement of the E8ms), one could see a variety of power on the La Junta-Denver trains. On August 18, 1970, F7A 259 and a steam generator car handle No. 191 at Colorado Springs. *Above and top right: Steve Patterson; bottom right: Larry White, collection of Joe McMillan.*

For the photographer, the Joint Line north of Colorado Springs is particularly scenic, especially Palmer Lake and north to Sedalia. Much of the railroad is accessible from state and county roads. For the northbound traveler, exit I-25 north of Colorado Springs at Monument and take State Route 105 west to Palmer Lake, then Douglas County 53 north to Larkspur, rejoining I-25 there. At Castle Rock, exit the Interstate and take U. S. 85, which will follow the railroad to Sedalia, Littleton and Denver.

Top left . . . SD45-2 5705 leads train 594 into the siding at Academy, 9.6 miles north of Colorado Springs, on March 18, 1983. The track leading out of the photo at left is a switching lead serving the U. S. Air Force Academy, for which the siding is appropriately named. The photo was taken from the engine of a southbound train holding the main track. *Bottom left* . . . Monument, Colorado is the next siding north of Academy. On October 8, 1975, train 414, behind F45 5918 and SD45-2s 5616-5675, waits at a red block for a northbound Santa Fe train to enter the siding. *Above* . . . Palmer Lake, 5.2 miles north of Monument, is a favorite spot for photographers. The rails bend sharply around the west side of Palmer Lake as they crest a steep grade. Southbound trains climb more than 2000 feet from Denver to Palmer Lake, and most trains require helpers, or "pushers," which usually cut out here and return to Denver. Palmer Lake lies at an altitude of 7,237 feet, the fourth highest elevation encounted by Santa Fe trains. On August 18, 1972, GP38 3533 (now 2333) leads southbound freight over the summit on Rio Grande rails. Before it was removed in the mid-1970s, Santa Fe's main line skirted the east side of the lake at right. The two tracks beside the train have since been removed. *Two photos left page: Bruce D. Barrett; above Robert R. Harmen.*

There is a mound of earth just off the highway at Palmer Lake whose summit is well trampled by the shoes of visitors. The mound, known locally as "Kodak Hill" for obvious reasons, is an excellent place from which to view or photograph trains. *Above* . . . On February 24, 1988, southbound QSN train Q-DVLJ behind GP39-2s 3431 and 3406 rounds the big curve at Palmer Lake with trailers for connecting QSN trains at La Junta. From the same mound at 2:55 p. m., August 25, 1986 . . . *below* . . . the camera records D&RGW SD50s 5517-5512-5510 and 95 empty coal cars returning north. *Above and below: Joe McMillan.*

Above . . . Four GE U28CGs lead an Air Force Academy football special at Palmer Lake on October 11, 1968. The deadhead passenger equipment has just arrived from the south and is stopped on the northward track. In a few minutes, the GEs will shove the train through a crossover to the southward track, run around the cars and depart for Academy, where cadets will board for the game. (At this time, there were still two main tracks south of Palmer Lake.) *Below* . . . F7A 261 leads an A-B-B-B set of "covered wagons" on southbound freight about a mile north of Palmer Lake on July 30, 1972. *Above: Jerry Porter; below: Robert R. Harmen.*

Above . . . An icy December day in 1989 finds SDFP45 100 piloting the northbound Q-LJDV into Palmer Lake. The QSN train is headed for Santa Fe's intermodal terminal at Big Lift, Colorado, 20 miles south of Denver. *Top right* . . . A set of four-motor units have hoisted southbound train 464 to Palmer Lake summit and now drift downgrade toward Monument and Colorado Springs. It's a beautiful February afternoon in 1987. *Bottom right* . . . If you were the engineer of a southbound train at Santa Fe mile 690 near Spruce on February 27, 1983, this would have been your chilly view! Spruce is a 2800-foot spur 2.5 miles north of Palmer Lake. The Rio Grande main, which accommodates northbound trains at this point, lies out of sight at left. *Above: Robert R. Harmen; top right: Robert S. Kaplan; bottom right: Steve Patterson.*

The Joint Line is an extremely complicated piece of railroad. When the Santa Fe built its line north from Pueblo to Denver in 1887, its tracks crossed over the Rio Grande on "flyovers" at three locations to obtain a more favorable grade. Following the AT&SF-D&RG paired trackage agreement, the flyovers were eliminated and the tracks realigned to form a more or less parallel route. Both the Santa Fe and the Rio Grande, therefore, own portions of each main line. For example, a southbound train out of Denver operates on D&RGW rails from South Denver to Sedalia, then over the Santa Fe to Spruce, Rio Grande to Kelker, Santa Fe to Crews, Rio Grande to D&RGW mile 86.5 and Santa Fe to Pueblo (Bragdon). On the D&RGW portions of each main track, the mileposts increase numerically southward, while on the Santa Fe portions, the mileage increases northward. The D&RGW dispatches southbound trains of both companies from South Denver to Palmer Lake and from Crews to Bragdon, while the AT&SF dispatches all northbounds from Bragdon to Crews and from Palmer Lake to South Denver. The Santa Fe also dispatches trains of both directions on the Rio Grande CTC-controlled single track between Palmer Lake and Crews. The Joint Line is also the only place on the Santa Fe where trains operate north and south in the timetable, as opposed to east and west over the rest of the railroad. Couple all this with steep grades, heavy coal trains and beautiful scenery and it's obvious that the Denver Subdivision is one of the most interesting on the railroad.

Above . . . Valentine's Day 1990 finds the 5843-5959-5960 (SD45-2/SDF45/SDF45) drifting downgrade from Palmer Lake with 20 empty grain hoppers while a southbound Burlington Northern train waits "in the sag" at Rio Grande mile 50 for a clear block. (Note the two unit Santa Fe pusher set at the rear of the BN train.) The old Spruce flyover was located in the distance where the tracks appear to converge. At this point, the grain train is on Santa Fe rails while the BN freight is on the Rio Grande. *Top right* . . . A pair of Santa Fe 5250 class SDF40-2s (ex-Amtrak SDP40Fs) help BN's Smithers Lake (Houston) coal loads up the steep grade between Spruce and Palmer Lake on March 4, 1988. *Bottom right* . . . Two GP20s handle a northbound work train at mile 687.5 north of Palmer Lake in July 1987. *Above: Dave Baker; two photos right page: Chuck Conway.*

Top left . . . Lots of fluffy white clouds add to the scene as the Q-DVLJ grinds upgrade near Palmer Lake behind SD40-2 5110 in March 1989. Douglas County Route 53, shown at the left of the train, closely follows the southward track through here. *Bottom left* . . . Greenland, Colorado, 2.7 miles north of Spruce, consists of a 1000-foot set out track off the southward main line at Santa Fe mileage 691.5. On February 7, 1988, merger-painted GP20 3074 leads train 424 by there en route to La Junta. *Below* . . . Famed Pikes Peak dominates the horizon as a pair of GP35s drift downgrade at mile 46 over East Plum Creek on Rio Grande rails at Greenland with the northbound Q-LJDV. The date is July 2, 1987. (Rio Grande's Greenland is also a short set out track, located at D&RGW mile 46.6. Note the southward main track visible in the distance over the top of the units.) *Below and top left: Chuck Conway; bottom left: John Rus.*

Above . . Three second generation EMDs curve beneath Castle Rock with northbound train 304 (Kansas City-Denver). The city of Castle Rock is located about 33 rail miles south of Denver. U. S. Highway 85 diverges from I-25 at this point and follows the railroad north. *Top right* . . . Burlington Northern unit coal trains are what today's Joint Line is all about. Counting both loads and empties, the route hosts 10 to 15 of these trains daily. Wyoming's Powder River coal destined for generating plants in Texas passes through Denver to Pueblo, then down the former C&S and FW&D lines into the Lone Star State. On August 6, 1985, BN C30-7 5506, under the responsibility of a Santa Fe crew, leads southbound coal loads into Sedalia. The track at right is the north end of a 4800-foot siding. *Bottom right* . . . The remains of a winter snow is visible in patches north of Sedalia at Rio Grande mile 23 as the Q-DVLJ rolls south behind a pair of GP39-2s. Barely discernable in this view is the Big Lift switcher coupled to the rear of the intermodal. The switcher had gone on duty earlier at Big Lift and, as usual, was hitching a ride on the rear of the Q-DVLJ to Colorado Springs where it would spend most of the day before returning north. (In this manner, the dispatcher would have to put up with only one train movement over the busy Joint Line instead of two.) *Above: Chuck Conway; two photos right page: Joe McMillan.*

Above . . . May showers threaten in the skies above Louviers, Colorado, four miles north of Sedalia, as train 424 gathers momentum for the long climb south to Palmer Lake. The date is May 25, 1985. *Below* . . . In December four years later, train 403 speeds through the snow at Acequia. GP30 2717, one of twenty-five 2700s that received the red, yellow and black merger scheme, will return to blue and yellow in six months. *Above and below: Chuck Conway.*

Above . . . Littleton, Colorado is a southern suburb of Denver at D&RGW mileage 10.3, if you're going south, or Santa Fe mileage 726.6, if you're heading north! On another threatening May day, GP30 2760 pilots train 444 south. In the late 1980s, the Rio Grande and Santa Fe main lines were realigned into a long trench through Littleton to avoid grade crossing congestion. City streets now pass safely overhead. *Below* . . . Santa Fe freights originate and terminate at BN's Denver yard. The trains operate over a portion of the First Subdivision of BN's Denver Division to reach the yard from the end of the Joint Line at South Denver, a distance of 5.1 miles. On March 15, 1989, SF30B 7200 pulls train 403 out of town on BN rails at South Park Junction, once a crossing with the famous C&S narrow gauge line to Climax and Leadville in the mountains west of Denver. *Above and below: Chuck Conway.*

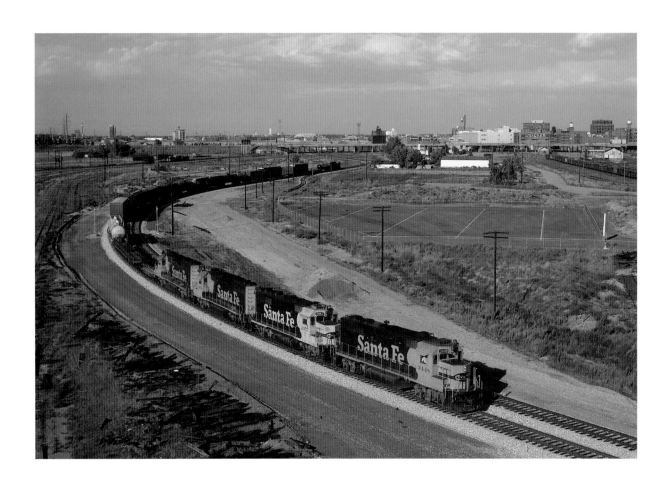

Above . . . Until late 1986, trains going south toward the Joint Line passed through Denver Union Terminal. Clearances between the trains and the platform canopies were tight, causing problems from time to time. SF30C 9520 passes by the venerable station on track 6 in October 1986 with southbound train 424. *Top left* . . . To alleviate close clearances and congestion, a new BN main line was constructed in late 1986 west of DUT in an open area once occupied by yard and industry tracks. On September 18, 1988, GP39-2 3448 and three mates wheel Kansas City train 403 over the new route. *Bottom left* . . . Two years earlier, on September 14, 1986, SD45-2 7201 guides southbound train 424 over a temporary Burlington Northern route through the remnants of BN's old 19th Street yard. This track was used until replaced by the new "corridor" line pictured above. Note the grading and track materials for the new main line at left. The lead unit of this consist was one of 30 former 5625 class locomotives remanufactured at San Bernardino in 1972 and 1973 emerging with 7200 series numbers designed to fit the numbering plan of the merged SP and AT&SF roster. After the merger was denied by the ICC in July 1986, units 7200-7229 became 5800-5829. The 7201—renumbered 5801—will lose its merger paint in February 1990. This photo was taken from the 16th Street Viaduct. *Above and bottom left: Thomas C. Byrnas; top left: John Rus; "Big Lift" trailer, top, Robert R. Harmen.*

Top left . . . Santa Fe No. 191 pulls out of Denver Union Terminal for La Junta on August 29, 1970 behind a tired and battle-worn F7A. The 238L would last another four years before retirement would catch up with the 20 year old unit. In December 1976, the primary components of the locomotive would be refashioned into CF7 2472 by craftsmen at Cleburne Shops. The passenger train would last just over eight months before its discontinuance with the coming of Amtrak. Denver's 15th Street viaduct—torn down in 1991—passes overhead. *Bottom left . . .* On August 13, 1968, after servicing at the CB&Q enginehouse north of DUT, E8m 81 is heading for the wye to be in position to power No. 191 out of Denver that afternoon at 3:30 p. m. Santa Fe rostered eight E8m cab units (80-87) and five boosters (80A-84A), all built in 1952 and 1953 using parts from the old 2 class E1s, built by EMC in 1937 and 1938. The thirteen E8ms were rated at 2000 h. p., rather than the normal 2250 h. p., hence the "m" for "modified" in the model designation. *Above . . .* Santa Fe train 424 accelerates out of Denver on the Joint Line just south of South Denver. At this point, the train is on D&RGW rails, while the passing northbound piggybacker is on the Santa Fe. Lead unit 8750 was one of a hundred U36Cs puchased by the railroad in 1974. Seventy of the 3600 h. p. GEs were rebuilt at Cleburne Shops to 3000 h. p. SF30Cs (9500-9569) in 1985 and 1986, which remain active in 1991. The rest of the 8700s—including the 8750—are stored out of service. *Top left: Steve Patterson; bottom left: Joe McMillan; above: John Rus.*

Just as this train is heading south and east, so will we. We bid farewell to Colorado and journey back to Emporia, Kansas and continue our trip south and west.

Our journey will now take us down the main line from Emporia, Kansas to Ellinor, then southwest through Wellington and northwest Oklahoma to the Texas state line. Along the way, we will also examine branch lines in southern and southwest Kansas and west central Oklahoma.

Above . . . Class Ce-1 caboose 999276 tags along behind train 581 entering the eastbound yard at Emporia on May 14, 1981. The train is on the long "electric lead" (so named because of the electric switches leading into the yard tracks from the lead) which leaves the south main track here at Merrick, 3.2 miles west of Emporia. *Below* . . . Nine years later, in September 1990, the 5970-5103-5055 (SDF45/SD40-2/SD40-2) power train 169 on the north main by abandoned Merrick tower. Note that the electric lead (as well as the eastbound yard), have been taken up. *Above: Lance F. Garrels; below: David P. Oroszi.*

Above . . . At 5:30 p. m., May 13, 1987, a pair of GE C30-7s cross over from the north to the middle main at Ellinor with train 195 (Chicago-Houston). In a few seconds the train will move from the middle track to the south main, which becomes the Emporia Subdivision main line to Welllington. Also at Ellinor, the north main becomes the Newton Sub main to Newton and west, and the middle main becomes the Emporia Sub siding. It sounds more complicated than it is. *Right* . . . Caboose 999147—on the rear of eastbound train 723—rumbles across an 840-foot pile trestle at mile 127.2, just south of Ellinor. The cantilever signal in the distance marks the west entrance to the Emporia Sub siding. *Above: David P. Oroszi; right: Lance F. Garrels; Ellinor station sign: David A. Franz.*

Above . . . At mile 129.2, near Gladstone, Kansas, Santa Fe rails pass over the Cottonwood River on an impressive structure. GE U23B 6338 leads train 305 over the bridge on December 26, 1977. The stone blocks in the foreground are remnants of the ill-fated construction attempts of the Kansas City, Mexico and Orient Railway through here in 1901. While considerable grading was done, no KCM&O rails were laid. We'll say more about the KCM&O later. *Below* . . . Just prior to noon on July 10, 1988, Texas-Chicago train 561 rounds a curve at mile 140, seconds before ducking under Kansas Route 177 west of Bazar. The bridge is a fine vantage point to view or photograph eastbound trains. *Above: David A. Franz; below: Joe McMillan.*

Above . . . SF30C 9529 and three EMDs on Kansas City to Texas freight 305 pass milepost 143 just east of Matfield Green on a hot afternoon in July 1988. *Below* . . . An hour earlier the same day, California train 189 behind a three-unit set of GP50s rounds the famed Matfield Green reverse curves at mile 143.2. In addition to being a great photo spot, Matfield Green is also the chigger capital of Kansas. If you're susceptible to bites from the little critters, be forewarned and be prepared! *Above and below: Joe McMillan.*

The Flint Hills, which run north to south across central Kansas, is the only extensive area of tall-grass prairie left in the eastern great plains. Rolling hills, marked by occasional rock outcroppings, are charteristic of the area. Abundant sources of flint rock are present, which once attracted western Kansas Indians needing the material for arrowheads, knives and spears. For the visitor to the Santa Fe, the area most associated with the Flint Hills is the portion of the Emporia Sub between Ellinor and Augusta, about 63 miles. In terms of curves and photographic locations, the best areas lie between Gladstone, mile 130.3 and Cassoday, mile 154.2. Most photography, however, is done within a few miles of the siding at Matfield Green. Kansas Route 177, between Strong City—on U. S. 50—and the I-35 interchange at Cassoday, is recommended for access to the area.

Left . . . A beautiful Kansas sunset sihouettes caboose 999009 tailing eastbound train 703 at Matfield Green on May 4, 1981. *Above* . . . Freshly clad in warbonnet dress, SDFP45 101 noses over Cook Street in Matfield Green on July 9, 1989 with eastbound pigs. The handsome unit was renumbered 92 in May 1990 and was still in active service in 1991. *Right: Lance F. Garrels; above: Steve and Cynthia Priest.*

137

Top left . . . A trio of merger-red units speed eastbound freight at Matfield Green on June 12, 1986. The signal in the background governs entry into the east end of the 7943-foot siding. (If a photographer standing at this location were to turn around and look north [timetable east], he or she would see the scene depicted on the bottom of page 135.) That's Kansas Route 177 at the left of the train. *Bottom left* . . . The east siding switch at Matfield Green on a late afternoon in October 1975 sets the scene as Bicentennial SD45-2 5703 rushes east with the *Super C*, the premium service speedster which ran between Chicago and Los Angeles from January 1968 to May 1976. At that time, the *Super C* carried symbols 198 and 891, which are still in use today on one of Santa Fe's most important trains. *Above* . . . F9A 287C and CF7 2635 are in command of Emporia-Arkansas City local No. 1311 west of Matfield Green in September 1974. Nicknamed the "oil local," the wayfreight spent most of its time around the oil refineries at El Dorado, and at Augusta, Mulvane and Winfield. The train no longer operates. *Top left: James L. Mitchell; bottom left and above: David A. Franz.*

The area between Matfield Green and Cassoday provides the visitor with some great panoramic views of the Flint Hills. *Above* . . . Chicago to Los Angeles train 168 rounds the big curve between miles 146 and 147 on February 13, 1982. If you have visited Kansas in the heat of the summer you wouldn't believe winter could come to this land, but it does! The lead unit, number 5427, was one of twelve SD45-2s (5426-5437) remanufactured at San Bernardino Shops from 1980 to 1982 with 3500 h. p. 16-cylinder prime movers. (SD45-2s are built with 20-cylinder engines rated at 3600 h. p.) All 12 units have since been retired or stored. *Top right* . . . SF30C 9559 (formerly U36C 8776) and two other GEs speed Chicago to Houston train 195 around Flint Hill curves west of mileage 148 on May 16, 1987. *Bottom right* . . . Aikman is a 14,338-foot siding 4.2 miles west of Cassoday. In August 1989, GE DASH 8-40B 7419 passes Aikman with train 188 for the West Coast. *Above: David A. Franz; two photos right page: James L. Mitchell.*

140

Below . . . You're looking over the roof of caboose 999550 tagging along behind train 981 at dawn on June 30, 1981 near Chelsea, Kansas, mile 165.5. *Top left* . . . El Dorado (pronounced EL-dor-AY-doh), located at mile 174.3, is the county seat of Butler County. El Dorado's fame began with an oil boom in 1915, and much of its industry is associated with the oil business. Two main tracks begin east of town and continue west through Augusta. In May 1976, an eastbound behind the 5702 waits on the south main track at a signal while a westbound diverges from single track to the north main. *Bottom right* . . . Train 308 rushes west on straight track at mile 170.6 east of El Dorado (geographically north) at 4:40 p. m., September 23, 1989. This is relatively new trackage. In 1980, Santa Fe rerouted about eight miles of main track through here to allow construction of the El Dorado Lake and dam. This line was built using concrete ties, as illustrated here. While there are other small test sections, this the largest concrete tie installation on the Santa Fe. This photo was taken from an overpass carrying an access road to the lake and recreation area. *Below: Lance F. Garrels; top right: Thomas C. Byrnas; bottom right: David P. Oroszi.*

The lines from Ellinor to Augusta, and from there to Wellington or Arkansas City, are the primary freight routes to the West Coast and Texas. The lines were built between 1877 and 1886 by Santa Fe construction companies beginning with a track linking Florence, Kansas (on the Emporia-Newton main line) with El Dorado. Lines were later built from there to Augusta and Winfield, and from Augusta to Wellington. In 1924, the Santa Fe improved the route by building a 47 mile cutoff from Ellinor to El Dorado, where the new line joined the old at DT Junction, mile 172.8. For many years, Tower B protected movements through the junction. The 18 mile Florence to El Dorado segment was abandoned in September 1942, but a portion of it still serves an industrial district in El Dorado. The Ellinor-Augusta-Mulvane-Wellington route was operated as the Fourth District of the Middle Division until May 15, 1988 when it became the Augusta Subdivision of the Illinois Division. In 1991, the Augusta and Ottawa Subs were combined and redesignated the Emporia Subdivision.

Augusta, Kansas, located at mile 185.7, is a major junction point. Most trains destined for Oklahoma City and Texas points curve off the Emporia Sub onto the Douglass Sub and head south through Winfield and Arkansas City. (Incidentally, in Kansas, "Arkansas" is pronounced ahr-KAN-zuhs, *not* ahr-kan-SAW. If you think you might embarrass yourself by mispronouncing "Arkansas City," be safe and call it what everybody else does: "Ark City.") While not the preferred route, Texas trains can also be routed west on the Emporia Subdivision 21 miles to Mulvane, then over the Arkansas City Sub to Winfield. (We will begin our journey down the Texas line on page 219.) *Above* . . . SDF45 5984 leads eastbound freight by mile 184 on the south main track east of Augusta on October 11, 1990. The rear of the train is crossing the 8th Subdivision of Burlington Northern's Springfield Division. This ex-Frisco branch runs from Pierce City, Missouri—on the Springfield to Tulsa main line—through Wichita to Buhler, Kansas. (The now-abandoned northwest end of this line [Buhler-Ellsworth] is discussed on pages 62 and 63 in connection with Santa Fe's Little River Subdivision.) Barely visible in the distance is the U. S. 54 overpass which spans the Santa Fe-BN crossing. Note the wye at the right of the train. *Top left* . . . Santa Fe's AG Tower protected the Frisco crossing at Augusta until it was closed in August 1979. In February 1980, westbound train 189 passes the structure seven months before it was torn down. *Bottom left* . . . At 10:00 a. m., May 16, 1987, SD45-2s 5845 and 5812 lead an eastbound through Augusta. At left, the rear of a Texas-bound train passes by on the Douglass Sub main. The attractive Augusta station, at right, still stands in 1991. *Above: Mel and Vern Finzer; top left: Lance F. Garrels; bottom left: David P. Oroszi.*

145

Mulvane, Kansas is another important junction town. The maze of tracks through and around this city can be confusing to the casual visitor. Two CTC-signaled main tracks begin at East Junction, mile 215.8, and run to West Junction, mile 222.0, on separate rights of way. Emporia Sub trains to Wellington can be routed around the east side of Mulvane on the south main track, or through town on the north main. The Arkansas City Sub, from Newton and Wichita, swings into the north main at mile 220, and in a short distance, diverges toward Winfield and Arkansas City. After the Ark City Sub leaves the north main, it passes under the south main track. (Frost, California, just west of Victorville, is the only other location on the railroad where one Santa Fe main line passes over another Santa Fe main line.) A train destined for Oklahoma City and the Gulf Coast is usually routed south at Augusta, as stated earlier. However, if the dispatcher lines it through Augusta to Mulvane, the train must be routed over the north track to be in a position to enter the Arkansas City Sub. At one time, the long branch line to Englewood, Kansas originated at Mulvane. The portion west of town was abandoned in August 1937. More on the Englewood Sub later.

Above . . . The 5001-5080-5179 (SD40/SD40-2/SD40-2) lead eastbound train 851 through Mulvane on the north main under an incredible sky in July 1987. The Arkansas City Sub main line to Winfield and Ark City diverges from the Emporia Sub just beyond the left cantilever signal. *Top right* . . . A pair of GP35s grace the point of a local at Mulvane in August 1985. The station has been converted to a museum and still stands in 1991. *Middle right* . . . Train 189 zips through a steel-arch tunnel under a rural road (95th Street South) at mile X216.3 on the south main at East Junction. The date is April 2, 1989. *Bottom right* . . . The south main track of the Emporia Subdivision passes over the Arkansas City Sub at Mulvane, providing a chance for a unique photo opportunity, if you are lucky!. (Use Central Street to get close to this location.) Eastbound train 843 passes overhead as QSN train Q-DVHO (Denver-Houston) scoots underneath on May 14, 1987. *Above, middle and bottom right: Fred Tefft; top right: Jim Primm.*

Top left . . . A short section of double track begins at Cicero, Kansas, mile 230.6, and runs west to SK Junction at Wellington. On August 19, 1989, "Super Fleet" SDFP45s 100 and 101, with GP50s 3830 and 3815 coupled behind, cruise east with train 971 (Richmond-Chicago) on the south track at Cicero. The photographer recorded this view from a rural overpass at mile 231.8. *Bottom left* . . . Nine months later, on May 24, 1990, another engine 100 leads the 2nd 891 near the same location. The hotshot is trailing the first eastbound run of the new 100 class GP60Ms (100-162), which were delivered from May to September 1990. Coupled to the 100 are SDFP45s 96 and 92, GP60M 101 and business car *Mountainair*—since renamed *John S. Reed*. The same engine combination had left Chicago westbound with train Q-NYLA on May 20, and is shown here returning. The 100 class SDFP45s had just been renumbered to the 90 class that month and interestingly, SDFP45 92 in this consist was the 101 shown in the top photo! This picture was taken off the overpass at mile 236.2 which carries U. S. 160 over the railroad. The grain elevator in the distance is located on the Moline Subdivision (Wellington to Chanute). The Moline Sub joins the main line at SK Junction, just out of sight at right. *Below* . . . Viewed from the U. S. 160 overpass, train 881 speeds east on a frosty December 14, 1987. *Three photos: Keel Middleton.*

Wellington is not only Superman's home, but it was also headquarters of the Panhandle Division until September 1, 1961 when the division was dissolved, its trackage going to the expanding Plains Division. Wellington is now the crew change point for Eastern Region trains operating between Kansas City and Amarillo. It is also the originating point for several local train assignments. While it is still an active location, Wellington is a mere shadow of its former self. Its importance has diminished considerably during the past decade. Most of its remaining mechanical facilities were razed between December 1990 and February 1991, and many jobs have been abolished.

Middle left . . . Wellington's yard still sees some activity. On January 17, 1990, floodlights cast an eerie yellow glow over the area as yard engine 2322 idles between assignments. *Bottom left* . . . A crewman detrains from SD40 5018 at Wellington in December 1980. *Above* . . . Caboose 999063 rests at the rear of an eastbound pausing at Wellington for a crew change and inspection in October 1968. A late afternoon thunderstorm has just drenched the town, and now the setting sun imparts brilliant hues to the western sky. *Middle left: Keel Middleton; Wellington sign and above: Joe McMillan; bottom left: Lance F. Garrels.*

Before continuing west, let's look briefly at the Santa Fe in southeastern Kansas.

Top . . . Operations of the old Southern Kansas Division were directed from this magnificent building in Chanute, Kansas. The structure was built during 1904 and 1905, and still stands in 1991. The Southern Kansas Division division was dissolved in 1948 and its trackage split between the Eastern and Oklahoma Divisions. *Right* . . . A roundhouse, locomotive shop and other supporting buildings were constructed at Chanute in 1908, but nearly all traces of them are gone today. This concrete coal chute, built in 1922, served the railroad for many years. It was photographed in November 1985, two years before it was torn down. Operations in Chanute have steadily declined since the end of the steam era. *Two photos Chanute station: Joe McMillan; right: Michael W. Blaszak.*

Santa Fe lines radiated from Chanute in four directions. The Leavenworth, Lawrence and Galveston Railroad built the original line south from Ottawa through Chanute to Coffeyville between 1869 and 1871. A successor company, the Kansas City, Lawrence and Southern, built west from Independence (at the end of a ten mile branch off the LL&G at Cherryvale) to Wellington, and on to Harper. The "Chanute Extension," built in 1886, connected Chanute with Longton on the Cherryvale-Wellington line, which then became part of the "main line" between Chanute and Wellington. This route was later designated the Fourth District, and in 1988, the Moline Subdivision. (The 24.2 mile Independence-Longton segment was abandoned in 1964.) The Girard District (Chanute to Pittsburg), built between 1884 and 1887, extended to Joplin, Mo. via trackage rights over the KCS. The 77.8 mile line was abandoned in 1986. The segment of the Tulsa line between Ottawa and Iola, 18 miles north of Chanute, was sold to the KCT Railway Corporation on May 2, 1990, and subsequently abandoned. The Moline and Coffeyville Subs, and the remaining portion of the Tulsa Sub, were sold to the South Kansas & Oklahoma Railroad on December 28, 1990. *Above* . . . LIL39 (Wellington to Chanute) crosses backwaters of the Arkansas River on bridge 255.7 east of Oxford, Kansas on April 17, 1989, and later . . . *below* . . . spans the Walnut River at Winfield, mile 247.4. *Above: Keel Middleton; below: Mel Finzer.*

153

The 43.1 mile Hunnewell District, running south out of Wellington to Tonkawa, Oklahoma, was built between 1880 and 1899. The branch crossed the old Anthony District (Anthony to Arkansas City) at South Haven and the H&S District at Blackwell. The H&S ran south from Hutchinson through Kingman, Harper, Anthony, Medford and Blackwell to Ponca City, Oklahoma, 141.9 miles. In the mid-1960s, the Blackwell-Ponca City segment of the H&S was redesignated as the Ponca City District and the Hunnewell District was made part of the H&S. (The Ponca City District was abandoned in November 1985 after the bridge across the Chikaskia River burned.) Between Blackwell and Wellington, an "X" was placed on the mileposts preceding the number to distinguish these mileposts from others of the same numbers on the north end of the district. The nine mile line from Blackwell to Tonkawa—the Tonkawa Industrial Spur—was sold in October 1989, but the promised rail service didn't materialize and the line was taken up. In 1991, the Wellington-Blackwell line was served tri-weekly by a local out of Wellington, which occasionally made side trips west on the H&S to Deer Creek.

Top left . . .GP35 2882 crosses the Chikaskia River (pronounced chuh-KAS-ki-uh) at mile X33 north of Blackwell on June 16, 1989. The short train is returning to Wellington after switching in Blackwell. *Bottom left* . . . Two months later, GP30 2773 tows three cars south near mile X32. During a humid August noontime . . . *below* . . . the 2773 switches the ConAgra flour mill in Blackwell, the principal industry on the branch. *Bottom* . . . The station at Braman, Oklahoma, located at mile X25.2, was built in 1899, probably by the Kansas Southeastern, one of three predecessor roads that built the line. The building, since razed, was photographed in July 1981, five months before the agency closed. The South Haven station was built by the Santa Fe in 1917 to replace an earlier structure. After closing, the building was moved to a private residence nearby. This photo was taken in September 1967. *Top left: Keel Middleton; bottom left, below and Blackwell station sign: Joe McMillan; Braman station: Jim Primm; South Haven: Howard Killam.*

Above . . . We return to Wellington and head west on the main track as the flying camera records the Medicine Lodge local leaving town on October 10, 1990. The wayfreight is crossing over "Rock Island Slough" and Union Pacific's OKT Subdivision (Wichita-Fort Worth), originally Rock Island's main line between Texas and the Twin Cities. After the demise of the CRI&P, the line was operated as the Wichita Subdivision of M-K-T's Oklahoma, Kansas and Texas Railroad until the Katy merged into the UP System in 1988. The small grain elevator nearest the horizon is the same elevator shown in the photo at the bottom of page 148. Wellington yard can be seen below and to the right of it. *Top right* . . . Old highway 160 crosses over the tracks on bridge 242.3 at Roland, the first siding west of Wellington on the Waynoka Subdivision. From that spot, train 326 is recorded climbing west out of Wellington on September 21, 1980. Note the interesting depot-like structure in the background. About 1974, a theme restaurant called Slate Creek Depot was constructed here using the Belle Plaine, Argonia and Sharon depots and a portion of the Mayfield depot. Unfortunately, the restaurant was destroyed by fire on July 26, 1982, and Slate Creek Depot was only a memory by September 1990 . . . *bottom right* . . . as Chicago-Richmond train 169 behind SDF45 5970 and two SD40-2s passes Roland. *Above: Mel and Vern Finzer; top right: Lance F. Garrels; bottom right: David P. Oroszi.*

Below . . If you had looked west from bridge 242.3 at Roland on July 26, 1990, you might have seen this view of train 891 topping the grade with a string of Chicago-bound trailers behind a foursome of new GP60Ms. Lead unit 142 had been on the property only 10 days when this photo was made. *Above . . .* A year earlier, in September 1989, a Speno rail grinding train backs slowly west at mile 242. The Santa Fe contracts with Speno to prolong its rail life by grinding away surface irregularities caused by the passing of trains. *Above and below: Keel Middleton.*

Above . . . GP20 3009 and GP30 2720 cross the Chikaskia River west of Argonia (ahr-GOHN-i-uh) at mile 260.5 with local train LKK43 en route to the Englewood Subdivision, April 17, 1989. *Below* . . . On a sunny September 21, 1988, red over green is the signal indication as your eastbound approaches the west siding switch at Mayfield, Kansas, mile 248, to meet train 308 (Kansas City-Barstow). *Above and below: Keel Middleton.*

Top left . . . A crewman off GP60M 140, at the point the 961 train at the east end of the Danville siding, mile 265.5, obeys rule 109 (inspection of passing trains) as train Q-LANY speeds by on the main track behind DASH 8-40B 7410. Barely visible in the distance is the U. S. 160 overpass. (U. S. 160 generally follows the main line west from Wellington to Attica, mile 285.) *Bottom left* . . . You're on the rear steps of caboose 999234 trailing train 981 in the siding at Danville meeting a westbound on the main line behind GP50 3816 on October 14, 1984. *Above* . . . At Harper, Kansas Santa Fe's H&S Subdivision, which runs north-south through town, crosses the main line through a series of crossovers west of the depot. Viewed from the Kansas Route 2 overpass on October 10, 1990, Englewood Sub local X-WLWK leaves the Harper siding and enters yard track No. 1. In just over a mile, the train will curve north onto the H&S main track. Trailing GP39-2 3686 and a pair of GE B23-7s are gondolas of gravel for a highway resurfacing project at Englewood. The track to the right of the siding is the Waynoka Sub main line, and the track to the right of it is an abandoned connection to the old KCM&O yard in Harper used by the Santa Fe until recently to serve several industries. *Two photos left page: Keel Middleton; Harper sign 7-11-88: Joe McMillan; above: Tom Carlson.*

We will leave the main line here and follow the H&S, Englewood, Wichita and Medicine Lodge Subdivisions before continuing west on page 183.

Above . . . LKK46 (Wellington-Kingman-Pratt) passes over the Chikaskia River just south of Rago, Kansas at mile 48. The train will continue north through Rago (RAY-goh) to Kingman, then work both ways out of there on the Wichita Sub. The date is April 20, 1989. *Below* . . . Six months later, ex-TP&W GP38-2 2375 idles on an H&S Sub work train at mile 12 near Castleton, Kansas. The train had brought up a pile driver from Kiowa and some ballast cars from Castleton for a bridge renewal project. The H&S Sub was built, appropriately, by the Hutchinson & Southern Railroad between 1889 and 1899. It was purchased by the AT&SF on December 20, 1899. *Above: Mel Finzer; below: Keel Middleton.*

Above . . . GP35 2916 and GP39-2 3423 rumble across a pile trestle over the North Fork of the Ninnescah River (NIN-uh-scah) west of Garden Plain on January 4, 1990. Garden Plain is on the Wichita Subdivision 20 miles west of Wichita (WICH-i-tah). The 44-mile segment between Wichita and Kingman was built in 1884 as the Wichita & Western. *Below* . . . Eight months later, on August 2, the 6376-3009-2319 (B23-7/GP20/GP38) switch the Garvey Elevator at Calista, 25 miles east of Pratt. The railroad west of Kingman was constructed as the Kingman, Pratt & Western, which commenced operation in 1887 to the west Kiowa County line, about 45 miles beyond Pratt. However, by 1898, the line had been cut back to Pratt, its present terminus. The KP&W was absorbed by the W&W in July 1889, which in turn was purchased by the AT&SF on December 31, 1898. *Above and below: Keel Middleton.*

Below . . . It's August 11, 1989 and local LKK46 has just tied up on the main track in front of the Kingman station after working all night. The train had left Wellington the previous evening, traveled west on the Waynoka Sub main to Harper, then north on the H&S to Kingman. From there, the local made a roundtrip to Garden Plain on the Wichita Sub, capping the day's work by derailing two hoppers on the north leg of the H&S Sub wye at Kingman. Tonight, the crew will travel west to Pratt before returning to Kingman and Wellington. *Top right* . . . In September 1989, a Wichita Sub work train with GP7 1325 crosses the Arkansas River in Wichita. Yard engines from Santa Fe's Wichita yard regularly serve this end of the branch to mile 9.

Of the several Santa Fe branch lines west of Wichita, the Englewood Subdivision is probably the most interesting. The 166 mile branch was built west from Mulvane in 1886 and 1887, passing through Viola and Rago to Englewood. Viola was also on the Fairview District (ex-KCM&O main line between Wichita and Harper). In August 1937, after the 22.7 mile Mulvane-Viola segment was abandoned, the Englewood District was served out of Wichita over the Fairview District to Viola, then west to Rago. In November 1979, heavy rains washed out the Ninnescah River bridge between Clonmel (KLAHN-mel) and Viola, severing the line. After this mishap, the only access to the Englewood District was from the H&S at Rago. The Wichita-Clonmel and Rago-Anness segments were operated on an as-needed basis until they were abandoned—Wichita to Clonmel in 1989 and Rago-Anness a year later. In 1991, the Englewood Subdivision consisted of 120.4 miles of track from mile 46 just east of Rago to mile 166.4 at Englewood. *Bottom right* . . . On January 2, 1990, local X-WLWK crosses backwaters of the Chikaskia River just west of Rago with a string of empty grain hoppers for elevators along the way. *Two photos this page: Joe McMillan; two photos right page: Keel Middleton.*

Above . . . The same train pictured on the previous page rumbles west at mile 59, just beyond Zenda, Kansas. On February 8, 1983 . . . *below* . . . GP38 3525 (now 2325) noses into snow as the two-unit consist backs into the west end of the elevator track at Zenda to switch Zenda Grain & Supply. Zenda, incidentally, was named after the popular novel *The Prisoner of Zenda*, written in 1894 by Anthony Hope Hawkins. *Right page* . . . The Englewood turn, symboled X-WLWL, had left Wellington on December 26, 1989, and now, two days later, it is passing over the Chikaskia River at mile 53 nearing Spivey. (The highway bridge on the other side of the trestle carries Kansas Route 42 over the river.) At Rago, the local will turn north on the H&S to Kingman, then east on the Wichita Sub to Garden Plain. After switching there, the train will journey west to Pratt before tying up for the night back at Kingman. The next morning, December 29, the turn will leave Kingman south on the H&S to Harper, then east to Wellington. In the early 1990s, it was typical for these three subdivisions to be served on as "as needed" basis by a single train out on line for four or five days. *Two photos this page: Keel Middleton; two photos right page: Fred Tefft.*

Above . . . In September 1990, three GP7s visited the Englewood Subdivision. GP7s see infrequent service on these branches—GP20s, GP30s, GP35s, GP38s, GP39-2s and B23-7s are regular power. Early on the morning of September 10th, the 2201-2188-2236 shove a hopper through the passing track at Sawyer for spotting at Sawyer Co-op on the other side of the main at right. After its work is completed, the train will continue west to Englewood, arriving there the next day (see page 176). *Top right* . . . Two days later, and now running east, the wayfreight greets a foggy sunrise at the east end of the Coats elevator track, mile 88. *Bottom right* . . . Walking out of the fog, a trainman inspects the brakes before departing Coats. The morning sun reflects off a freshly painted 2201. *Three photos: Keel Middleton.*

Photographing the Englewood Subdivision, as well as the Wichita and H&S Subs, can be difficult and frustrating. In the past, all three subdivisions had regularly assigned locals with schedules that were somewhat predictable, depending upon the season. Grain and farm-related products are the mainstay of these lines and service was tailored to meet seasonal needs. In addition to the assigned locals, it was not unusual to see extra trains operating during the grain harvest to handle the increased business. Times have changed, however, and there are no more regularly assigned wayfreights on these branches. Instead, as mentioned earlier, one train originating at Wellington usually serves all three subdivisions at the same time with no predictable route or schedule. The trains wander from one subdivision to another as work dictates, tying up for rest where the "hog law" catches the crew. To further complicate matters for the photographer, the freights generally run at night in the heat of the summer, usually going on duty about 10 p.m. Photography is possible only from sunrise until the trains stop for the day, usually before noon. The best time to visit these three branches is during the late fall, winter or early spring when the trains are on their daylight schedules.

Top left . . . The track geometry car spends most of its time riding the main line, but occasionally it sees more mundane duties. It's late in the afternoon on May 2, 1984, and the train crew has just gone "dead on the law" at Sawyer after a long day with the work train. Car 85—converted in 1973 from business car 39—measures track characteristics while rolling at speed across the railroad. The Sawyer station, built in 1887 and remodeled in 1921, was closed in September 1982 and later moved to a site along Kansas Route 42. *Bottom left* . . . Springvale, Kansas is located at mile 95.1, fifteen miles west of Sawyer. On March 13, 1983, B23-7 6382 moves west with only the waycar in tow. (The quaint elevator burned in the mid-1980s.) *Above* . . . The engineer's first view of the morning sun after traveling on the Englewood Sub all night. The location is milepost 93, two miles east of Springvale, and the date is September 1990. *Top left and above, Keel Middleton; bottom left: Lee Berglund.*

Below . . . Belvidere, Kansas is located at mile 104.4 in the Medicine River valley. On October 10, 1990, a westbound local with a consist of gravel and empty grain hoppers passes through town behind three GE B23-7s. Trains from either direction descend over 200 feet in elevation approaching Belvidere, cross the river (in the treeline around the curve in the distance) and ascend the grade beyond. Note the wye, barely visible to the right of the train. The track next to the engines is a 2690-foot passing siding. The Medicine Lodge Subdivision joins the Englewood Sub at OB Junction, mile 103.3, just east of the Medicine River bridge. (We'll visit the Medicine Lodge Sub beginning on page 178.) *Top right* . . . Probably the most scenic part of the Englewood Sub lies between Belvidere and Wilmore, especially around mile 108. The rails curve and climb west out of the Medicine River valley to an elevation of 2140 feet at mile 120.5, the highest point on the line. On June 23, 1984, U23B 6327 and a pair of EMDs lead a string of grain hoppers west near mile 108. *Bottom right* . . . A trackside grave lies on the south side of the right of way at mile 107. While stories vary, it is apparently the resting place of a Mexican track worker killed during the construction of the railroad. *Below* . . . *Mel and Vern Finzer; top right: Jim Primm; Bottom right: Keel Middleton.*

Above . . . Coldwater, Kansas, mile 125, is a common tie up point for trains operating over the Englewood Subdivision. On July 7, 1984, four units idle on the main track while the crew rests at a nearby motel. That night, they will reassemble their train and amble east at 20 m. p. h., the maximum allowable speed on the subdivision. The Coldwater station was a large 24' x 92' structure when built in 1887, but 19' was removed from this end and 22' from the other end in 1943. The agency was closed in September 1982 and the building moved off site. (The farm lands of western Kansas are well populated with ex-Santa Fe station buildings.) *Top right . . .* Under threatening clouds, GP20 3050 powers a work train west of Protection in May 1989. The material in the two air dumps behind the locomotive will be used to fill a track washout. *Bottom right . . .* You are looking west from a boxcar perch at GP20s 3108 and 3152 switching grain hoppers in the passing track at Protection, Kansas, mile 134.7. The main line lies to the left of the units. *Above: Jim Primm; top right: Keel Middleton; bottom right: David K.Webb.*

Above . . . Local X-WLWK, behind the same GP7s pictured earlier, prepares to depart Englewood on September 11, 1990 with a string of empty gravel gons. The gondolas will return to Wellington, then move east over the Moline Subdivision (now South Kansas & Oklahoma Railroad) to a quarry near Moline. The elevator at left marks the very west end of the subdivision. *Below* . . . GP20 3064 leads grain hoppers east of Acres (mile 158.8) toward Ashland in June 1984. *Above: Keel Middleton; below Jim Primm.*

From Englewood, we return to the H&S Subdivision at Anthony, Kansas, 9.7 miles south of Harper. The same trains that serve the rest of the H&S, Wichita and Englewood Subs occassionally make side trips down from Harper to serve customers at Anthony. While H&S Sub trackage is still in place south and east of here, it is rarely used between Anthony and Deer Creek. (The east end of the subdivision is served by a local out of Wellington. See pages 154 and 155.) Anthony was the western terminus of the 59.5-mile Anthony District which ran east to Arkansas City. This railroad was built as the Kansas Southwestern and originally was jointly owned with the Frisco. In 1936, the 6.7 mile segment between Geuda Springs and Ark City was abandoned after floods destroyed the Chikaskia River bridge. The rest of the line was abandoned in parts with the last segment—Anthony to Metcalf, 16.3 miles—going in March 1986. *Below* . . . On October 4, 1982, B23-7 6381 plows dirt at a road crossing east of Anthony while returning cab-hop from Bluff City. A track inspector in a hy-rail truck follows the slow-moving train. *Above* . . . GP35 2932 and B23-7 6404 switch an elevator on the east side of the Anthony station in November 1989. The H&S Sub passes by on the west side of the building. The 1928 brick structure is now a museum. *Above: Keel Middleton; below: Michael A. Blaszak.*

Attica, Kansas is located on the Waynoka Subdivision main line 11.8 miles west of Harper. *Top left* . . . On April 4, 1990, the 5862 leads westbound pigs through town. The track to the left of the train is the east end of the north siding. Yard track No. 1 is in the immediate foreground. Attica is the junction point with the 50.6-mile Medicine Lodge Subdivision which runs west from here to a connection with the Englewood Sub at OB Junction near Belvidere. (The west end of the branch between mile 41 and OB Junction is no longer used.) The switch leading to the Medicine Lodge Sub lies immediately behind the photographer. *Above and bottom left* . . . It's late in the afternoon on August 9, 1989 at Medicine Lodge as GP38 2339 and GP39-2 3615 on local LKK54 idle in the bright sun while the crew has supper at a nearby restaurant. Unlike the neighboring H&S, Wichita and Englewood Subdivisions, the Medicine Lodge branch does not depend solely upon grain and farm products for its existence. Most of the line's revenue comes from a large wallboard plant at Medicine Lodge operated by Gold Bond Building Products, a division of National Gypsum. The AT&SF handles outbound loads of finished products and shuttles raw material to the plant from a large gypsum quarry and mine near Sun City, about 20 miles west of Medicine Lodge. After the crew returns from supper, their first chore will be to switch the Gold Bond plant. They will then depart for Sun City with empty hoppers for the mine. In the early hours of the morning, the local will return to Medicine Lodge with a string of gyp hoppers, switch the plant and tie up. The next afternoon, the crew will go on duty and reverse the process, tying up back in Wellington early the next morning. *Top left: Mel Finzer; bottom left and above: Joe McMillan.*

179

Top left . . . A spring snow in March 1984 blankets the countryside as the Medicine Lodge local switches gyp hoppers at the National Gysum quarry and mine. The mine is at the end of a two mile spur off the main line at mile 40.3, just west of Sun City. Switching here is not easy. Handling the heavy cars on the 2 percent grade calls for caution on the part of the crew. On a much warmer day three months later . . . *bottom left* . . . the local pauses at the Sun City station before heading up to the mine. Note the gyp hoppers in the siding and house track. The Sun City depot had closed the previous year and would later be moved off site. *Below* . . . At 7:30 p. m. on August 10, 1989, LKK54 drifts into Sun City behind the "Son City" Whosoever Welcome church. *Top left: Keel Middleton; bottom left: Jim Primm; below: Joe McMillan.*

Bottom left . . . GP39-2 3665 has obviously met some chilly resistance while working the Medicine Lodge District in February 1982. The pilot plow, located on the other end of the locomotive, might have made the journey easier had the locomotive operated front first. *Top left . . .* Eight years later, in April 1990, the Medicine Lodge local heads into the sunset nearing Sharon, Kansas, located midway between Attica and Medicine Lodge.

Kiowa, Kansas is located on the Kansas-Oklahoma border, 21.3 miles west of Attica on the main line. Its handsome station . . . *below* . . . was built in 1915 to a unique set of plans. The agency closed in August 1983, but the building was still being used in 1991 by company maintenance of way forces. *Above* . . . The last day of 1980 finds SD45-2 5714 stopped on the main track at mile 309, just west of Kiowa, as SD45 5581 leads westbound piggybacks through the Kiowa siding. The 5581 was rebuilt in December 1983 to cabless booster unit 5501. Both it and the 5714 remain in service in 1991. *Top left: Mel Finzer; bottom left: Keel Middleton; above: Kenneth B. Fitzgerald; below: Lee Berglund.*

Before continuing west on the main line, let's look at two interesting Santa Fe branch lines in Oklahoma: the Enid and Altus Subdivisions. The 116.9 mile Enid Sub runs southeast from a junction with the main line at Kiowa through Enid to Guthrie, Oklahoma, where it ties into the Arkansas City-Oklahoma City main line. *Above* . . . On an rainy August 1989 morning, Kiowa-Enid local LKO96 slows to a stop at Cherokee, Oklahoma, 20 miles out of Kiowa. The local will pick up several locomotives off the stock track that had been damaged earlier in a derailment on the Altus Sub. *Below* . . . The photographer is nearly too late to shoot a train passing the Burlington station. The Kiowa-Enid local passes the doomed structure on June 20, 1987. *Above: Joe McMillan; below: Lee Berglund.*

From Cherokee, the Enid Sub traverses the barren salt flats along the edge of the Great Salt Plains State Park and wildlife refuge before crossing U. S. Highway 64 and curving into Jet, Oklahoma. Jet, named for the town's first postmaster, is well known in the region as the gateway to the Great Salt Plains and take-off point for those who dig for rare selenite crystals in the nearby gypsum flats. *Below . . .* The Kiowa-Enid local switches at Jet in September 1980 before continuing east. Nash, Oklahoma, located 8.2 miles east of Jet . . . *bottom . . .* was home to this attractive station when photograped in May 1974. The buildings at both Jet and Nash have since been removed. *Below: Lee Berglund; Jet sign (8-11-89) and Nash station: Joe McMillan.*

Probably one of the best photo locations on the Enid Subdivision is a rural overpass at mile 36.3—on the border between Grant and Alfalfa Counties—about half way between Jet and Nash. *Below* . . . The 2727-2351-6384 (GP30/GP38/B23-7) lead local LKO95 westbound on August 11, 1989. *Above* . . . A misty rain darkens the scene at the same location the next morning as eastbound LKO96 labors up a short 0.60% grade. At this time, the trains were regularly assigned and operated tri-weekly out of Enid. Shortly after these photos were taken, however, locals LKO95 and LKO96 were abolished following the implementation of a trackage rights agreement with the Burlington Northern between Enid and Avard. In 1991, the Enid-Kiowa line was being operated on an as needed basis, usually about twice a month. *Both photos: Joe McMillan.*

The words "Enid" and "grain" are synonymous. Enid has long been Oklahoma's most important center for the storing, processing and marketing of grain. Enid is also the county seat of Garfield County, one of the nation's greatest wheat producers. Hundreds of Santa Fe unit grain trains originate here and travel east down the Enid Sub to Guthrie, then south to the Gulf Coast. Depending on the season and marketing conditions, Enid can be a very busy place. The Enid-Kiowa local pulls out of the Enid yard . . . *above* . . . on July 27, 1987. In a quarter mile, the local will curve onto Burlington Northern's 7th Subdivision (Fort Worth Division) and run to Blanton, a distance of three miles. In February 1982 . . . *below* . . . a brakeman closes the BN switch at Blanton after the westbound local has cleared the ex-Frisco trackage. BN's 7th Sub main line runs from Tulsa's Cherokee Yard 175 miles west to Avard on Santa Fe's Waynoka Sub. This is the route of several AT&SF-BN run through trains, such as the Q-BHLA (Birmingham-Los Angeles) and its counterpart, Q-LABH. In June 1989, the Santa Fe and BN entered into a joint track arrangement permitting Santa Fe to operate its own trains over the route. Through railcars now make up Santa Fe trains 476 (westbound) and 674 (eastbound) which are scheduled daily between Oklahoma City and Waynoka via Enid and Avard. *Above: Joe McMillan; below: Kenneth B. Fitzgerald.*

One of the most interesting Santa Fe branch lines in Oklahoma was the old Kansas City, Mexico and Orient main line running southwest from Cherokee—on the Kiowa-Enid line—to Altus, Oklahoma, and continuing through Hamlin and Sweetwater to Maryneal, Texas, a distance of 357.8 miles. This book will examine the north end of the "Orient," as it was often called. In the mid-1980s, Fairview, Oklahoma, 36 miles south of Cherokee, was still an on duty point for assigned locals working on what was then the Altus District of the Plains Division. *Above* . . . B23-7 6352 and U23B 6344 idle in the darkness on an August evening in 1978. As with many local train assignments in Kansas and Oklahoma, this train would go on duty at night during the summer months. In the station nearby, train order operator Joe Velasquez copies orders for the crew who will report for duty at 10 p. m. for Fairview-Clinton local 2213. Fairview's ex-KCM&O station is now preserved at the Major County Historical Complex east of town. *Above: Joe McMillan.*

From the connection with the Enid Subdivision at Cherokee, the ex-KCM&O line runs south through Yewed ("Dewey" spelled backwards), and Carmen, where the tracks cross BN's 7th Subdivision (Tulsa-Avard), to the Cimarron River bridge at Orienta. *Above* . . . Clinton-bound local LKO59, behind GP39-2 3442 and GP20 3004, crosses the Cimarron, 28 miles south of Cherokee, on January 19, 1989. *Below* . . . A southbound local crosses the Canadian River north of Thomas, Oklahoma on April 20, 1979. *Bottom left* . . . Longdale, 11.6 miles south of Fairview, is the setting as three EMDs lead southbound freight through fresh snow toward Clinton in February 1986. *Above: Keel Middleton; below: Jim Primm; bottom left: Kenneth B. Fitzgerald.*

Thomas, Oklahoma was located at mile 378.8, about halfway between Cherokee and Altus. Its station was moved here in 1946 from Rome, Kansas—seven miles south of Wellington on the H&S Sub—to replace an existing ex-KCM&O structure. The Santa Fe had trackage rights over a 12.8 mile segment of Frisco's Enid Subvivision (Enid-Davidson) from Foley, 7.2 miles south of Thomas, to Ewing, just north of Clinton. The agent at Thomas communicated with both the AT&SF and Frisco dispatchers, and issued Frisco train orders to southbound Santa Fe trains operating over the joint track. (Clinton cleared northbound trains.) Nothing remains of this location today except for a concrete floor slab. *Three photos, August 9, 1978: Joe McMillan.*

Above . . . Northbound LPL18 crosses the North Canadian River at Canton, Oklahoma at 2:35 p. m. on December 21, 1988. Four hours earlier . . . *below* . . . the same train crosses a trestle at mile 384, two miles north of Foley. GP39-2 3429 and GP35 2876 head the Cherokee-bound local. *Both photos: Joe McMillan.*

In the late 1890s, Arthur E. Stilwell, a Kansas City real estate and insurance executive, dreamed of connecting Kansas City with the Gulf of California by building a railroad southwest through Kansas, Oklahoma, Texas and across northwestern Mexico to Topolobampo, a potiential port site on the Gulf in the Mexican state of Sinaloa. Stilwell's new railroad, the Kansas City, Mexico and Orient, would open Kansas City to trade with the Orient by way of a rail line approximately 500 miles shorter than a route built directly to the Pacific Coast. His grandiose plan was announced to leading citizens in Kansas City on February 10, 1900. While some grading was done between Emporia and El Dorado, Stilwell decided to begin his railroad at Wichita and build southwest from there. (He planned to complete the Kansas City-Wichita segment later.) Construction actually started at Anthony, Kansas, where materials had been stockpiled. By November 1904, the KCM&O had connected Wichita and Fairview with a line passing through Viola, Harper, Anthony and Cherokee. The line was completed to Altus, Oklahoma in 1908, and to San Angelo, Texas a year later. By June 1913, the railroad had reached Alpine in west Texas, 227 miles west of San Angelo. Construction across Mexico was also underway during these years, but the harsh terrain and political upheavals prevented completion of the line until November 1961. The KCM&O fell on hard times in the 1920s. The railroad could not reach its full potiential until completed, and a lack of capital prevented that. There just wasn't enough revenue to keep the railroad operational, much less to complete it. A 1925 oil boom in west Texas helped, but it only delayed the inevitable. The KCM&O shopped around for a new owner and the Santa Fe acquired the property through a lease on August 1, 1929.

After the Santa Fe assumed control of the KCM&O, it extended the route from Alpine to Presidio to connect with the Mexican line. (By 1939, however, Santa Fe had sold the Mexican properties of the former Orient.) The AT&SF abandoned the former KCM&O main line between Anthony and Cherokee, a distance of 34 miles, in 1942, and removed the Wichita-Harper segment in several stages between 1961 and 1989. (The KCM&O track between Harper and Anthony was retained and remains in service today as part of the H&S Sub.) The 60 miles between Maryneal and San Angelo, Texas was torn up in 1982. Other than these changes, Stilwell's route remains essentially as he dreamed it ninety years ago. Unfortunately, the bonanza he anticipated never developed. The U. S. portion of the Orient was always a marginal line despite Santa Fe's efforts to develope business. On May 31, 1991, the Santa Fe sold the north end of the Orient, from Maryneal, Texas to Cherokee, Oklahoma to the Texas and Oklahoma Railroad.

Clinton, Oklahoma is another one of those small towns with a complicated track arrangement that can confuse the causal visitor. Clinton was once served by three major railroads: the Santa Fe, Rock Island and Frisco. CRI&P's Memphis-Oklahoma City-Amarillo line—the route of the *Cherokee* and *Choctaw Rockette*—passed by the north edge of town. The Farmrail System (FMRC) now operates a 46 mile section of this line from Elk City through Clinton, its headquarters, to Weatherford. The Grainbelt Corporation (GNBC), under the same management, operates the ex-Frisco (later BN) Enid-Davidson route. The north-south GNBC line passes through Clinton just east of the downtown area. Santa Fe's Altus Sub diverged from the GNBC at Ewing, 2.2 miles north of Clinton, crossed the Washita River, passed over the FMRC and skirted the west side of town. One leg of a wye just north of the FMRC crossing led to Santa Fe's old downtown station, which still stands in 1991. *Above* . . . Looking west, a pair of GP30s pass over Farmrail tracks at Clinton on May 26, 1989. U. S. Highway 183 spans the tracks in the background. Looking the opposite direction two years prior . . . *below* . . . an eastbound Farmrail train behind attractively-painted GP9 297 approaches the Santa Fe bridge as merger-painted B23-7s 6374 and 6373 pass overhead. The GNBC connects to the FMRC through those switches just visible between the legs of the Clinton sign. *Left* . . . Local LPL18 passes milepost 383 north of Custer City—seen in background—with nine cars for Cherokee on December 21, 1988. *Left: Joe McMillan; above: Lee Berglund; below: Keel Middleton.*

Santa Fe's new Clinton station lies in the southwest quadrant of town. Just south of that location, AT&SF's 136.6 mile Clinton to Pampa, Texas branch, the old "COW Line" (Clinton and Oklahoma Western Railway) tied into the Altus District. The COW was built between 1910 and 1931, and abandoned in October 1981. We will explore this line in Volume 3 of the Santa Fe in Color Series. *Top left* . . . a trio of four-motor units idle near the Clinton station at 10:30 P.M., January 4, 1988. Clinton had an open station until the Altus Subdivision was sold to the Texas and Oklahoma Railroad in May 1991. This building, new in 1980, is now the operational center for that regional railroad. *Below* . . . The long lens records LPL20 bouncing over 20 m.p.h. track at Milepost 414, six miles north of Dill City, Oklahoma. The local will reach Clinton in 13 miles and tie up for the night. The trestle in the foreground carries the rails over West Boggy Creek. *Bottom left* . . . Lone Wolf, named for a Kiowa Indian chief, lies at mile 440.9, 40 miles south of Clinton. Santa Fe's ex-KCM&O tracks passed to the east of town about a mile, crossing Rock Island's Chickasha-Mangum branch (Subdivision 26A of the Southern Division). After the demise of the Rock Island in March 1980, Santa Fe began to serve the Rock's Lone Wolf customers over a short segment of the branch. In December 1988, LPL20 is shown on the ex-CRI&P line approaching the crossing after switching a grain elevator in town. Caboose 999385 is on the Altus Sub main line. The cars on the right are on the interchange track between the two lines. *Top left: Michael W. Blaszak; bottom left and below: Joe McMillan.*

In the mid-1980s, the Altus Subdivision was served by a 6-day local originating at Wellington, Kansas. LPL15 would depart Sunday mornings, run west on the main line to Kiowa, then down the Enid Sub to Cherokee where it would curve south onto the Altus Sub, tying up for the night at Fairview. On Mondays, the train would run to Clinton as LPL17, and on Tuesdays to Altus as LPL19. The process was then reversed until the train returned to Wellington late Friday. After the closing of Fairview in 1988, local train LPL17 went on duty at Cherokee on Sunday afternoons and traveled south to Clinton. On Mondays, LPL19 ran from Clinton to Altus, returning as LPL20 on Tuesday evenings. By Wednesday night, LPL18 had tied up back at Cherokee. On Thursdays, LPL17 would travel to Clinton and return to Cherokee Friday night. The train symbols changed twice since that time in keeping with various operational reorganizations, but in general, the Altus Sub was operated in this manner until it was sold.

The deep rock cut south of Lugert between mile 449.5 and 449.9 is certainly not the typical terrain one might expect to see in Oklahoma. Between Lugert and Blair, Altus Subdivision rails parallel the south shore of Lake Altus for a short distance, then pass through an arm of the Quartz Mountains before they return to the familiar flat topography of the region. *Top left* . . . Local LPL20 approaches the rock cut en route north in December 1988. *Bottom left* . . . The 6415-2762-2815 (B23-7/GP30/GP35) lead an extra north (timetable direction east), symbol X-WLWL, through the cut in February 1987. Oklahoma Route 44 follows the railroad through here, but the highway goes over the rocks while the rails go through them. This photo was taken from a point near the road. *Above* . . . In April 1979, the Altus to Fairview local—then numbered 2214—eases through the cut at restricted speed. Timetable instructions warned train crews to pass through here "prepared to stop short of dirt or rock slides." *Top left: Joe McMillan; bottom left: Keel Middleton; above: Jim Primm.*

Top and middle left . . . LPL20 rounds the south end of Lake Altus on December 20, 1988. Oklahoma Route 44 is in the distance of the top photo at the left of the tracks. The deep cut is located down from the point where the highway turns back to the left (above the first car in the train). *Bottom left* . . . A few minutes prior to entering the cut, the local crosses the North Fork of the Red River on a long bridge. *Above* . . . On a December morning in 1988, the early morning rays illuminate GP35 2876 and GP39-2 3429 on the main track at Altus. The crew had arrived from Clinton the night before, switched their train and tied up. At 11:05 a.m. this morning, the train will leave town heading north with three loads, seven empties and the caboose. Hollis & Eastern CF7 2520 (ex-AT&SF 2520) idles in the background. The H&E is a 15 mile shortline—once a part of M-K-T's old Altus-Wellington, Texas branch—running west to the Republic Gypsum Company plant at Duke, producer of wallboard and other building products. The H&E connected with the Santa Fe and BN at Altus. *Below* . . . The nose of GP35 2876 is visible through the doorway of an abandoned M-K-T yard office in Altus. *Five photos: Joe McMillan.*

Top left . . . A sunny morning in July 1988 finds us back on the main line west of Alva, Oklahoma as a train of loaded grain hoppers, symbol G-NWAM (Newton to Amarillo), storms upgrade out of the Salt Fork River valley. The track at the right of the train is the 18,966-foot Noel siding which runs west from Alva to Noel. This photo was taken from the U. S. Highway 64 overpass at mile 327.5 on the southwest outskirts of Alva. *Bottom left* . . . A quick finger on the camera shutter was necessary to record this meet at mile 327.2 with Richmond-bound train 189. The photo was made from the cupola of a caboose trailing an eastbound in the Noel siding on May 7, 1985. *Above* . . . On

September 20, 1989, eastbound train 871 flies by a Speno rail grinding train at the east end of Noel siding, which is almost in downtown Alva. Located a mile behind the photographer is Alva's attractive 1909 station building. South of the station is a maze of industry tracks serving local businesses, including several on a remnant of Rock Island's former Subdivision 25C (Southern Division) which ran to Alva from North Enid, a distance of 71.5 miles. After Rock Island ceased operating in 1980, the Santa Fe began serving these CRI&P customers. *Right* . . . Capron is located 8.3 miles east of Alva. Its tiny station was moved here in 1903 from Huckle, Kansas (on the Englewood Sub). The building is now located in a field north of Alva. *Top left: Joe McMillan; bottom left and above: Keel Middleton; right: Lee Berglund.*

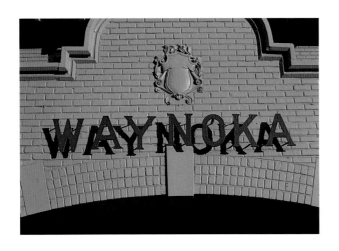

From Alva, main line rails continue southwest to Avard, where Burlington Northern's 7th Sub (Tulsa-Avard)—formerly Frisco's Perry and Avard Subs—swings in from the east. In 1991, about six daily run-through trains were interchanged between AT&SF and BN at Avard. Enid-based BN crews operate these trains east of Waynoka. Santa Fe trains 476 and 674 (Waynoka-Oklahoma City) operate over the BN between Avard and Enid, then over the Santa Fe to Oklahoma City. These two trains are manned by Santa Fe crews. The "Avard Gateway" was established with the Frisco in August 1973. Prior to that time, the AT&SF and Frisco—via subsidary Quannah, Acme and Pacific—swapped trains at Floydada, Texas in the Texas Panhandle.

Waynoka, Oklahoma is located at mile 345.5, 9.8 miles west of Avard. Until September 3, 1986, it was the crew change point between the First and Second Districts of the Plains Division. On that day, train and engine crews began running through between Wellington and Amarillo, 314 miles, one of Santa Fe's longest main line crew districts. The only crews changing here now are those operating the run-through trains. (Local train crews also go on and off duty at Waynoka.) Today, Waynoka is the dividing point between the Waynoka and Panhandle Subdivisions of the Eastern Region. *Middle left . . .* Waynoka's impressive station buildings are pictured in April 1987. The nearest building, built in 1910, was originally a Harvey House dining room, one of a chain of hotels and eating establishments along the Santa Fe Route whose mission was to bring good food and civilization to the developing west. After the Harvey House closed in 1937, the building was converted into a "reading room" (Santa Fe parlance for crew quarters) to house train and enginemen until the crew run-throughs were implemented in 1986. When the station—shown beyond the reading room—closed in 1978, its offices were moved to the crew quarters. Maintenance of way and signal forces were also located in the reading room. On September 20, 1991, the building was vacated and all activity is now based out of a small building nearby. The station building, incidentally, is now a museum. *Bottom left . . .* Frisco SD45 924 idles in front of the station on October 12, 1980, 40 days before becoming a BN locomotive. *Above . . .* As viewed from an eastbound, BN-AT&SF run-through train Q-BHLA (Birmingham-Los Angeles) approaches the Broadway crossing east of the station. At right, the Amarillo-Waynoka local moves down the yard lead. *Below . . .* GP7 2854, assigned to the Buffalo District local, idles across from the station on June 7, 1975. *Waynoka station sign, middle left and below: Lee Berglund; Waynoka Rails sign: Joe McMillan; bottom left: Kenneth B. Fitzgerald; above: Keel Middleton.*

The 52.2 mile Buffalo District was completed in July 1920 as the Buffalo Northwestern. It ran northwest out of Waynoka, generally following the Cimarron River. The line served an agricultural area, but it was never very profitable. On July 15, 1983, the branch was abandoned and its rails were lifted shortly thereafter. *Top left* . . . Weeds polish the pilot of F7A 252C as it leads a Waynoka-bound Buffalo District train at Selman, Oklahoma, eight miles from Buffalo, on January 15, 1972. *Middle left* . . . The end of the branch was near when the Buffalo depot was photographed in March 1982. *Bottom left* . . . Officials hy-rail at the base of the bluffs along the Cimarron River near Freedom the same month to prepare the company's case for abandonment of the Buffalo District. *Top left: Lee Berglund; middle and bottom left: Michael W. Blaszak.*

From Waynoka, Panhandle Subdivision rails cross the Cimarron River at mile 348.5 and curve south and west out of the valley. *Above* . . . At 11:08 a. m., August 9, 1987, train V-KCLA rounds a curve at Heman, Oklahoma, 5.6 miles west of Waynoka. ("V" symbol trains primarily transport motor vehicles and auto parts.) Two years later, on September 29, 1989 . . . *below* . . . SDFP45 102 leads train 199 around the big curve between Heman and Belva. Bending the rails through 136 degrees of curvature, this 2.6-mile curve is the longest curve on the Chicago-Los Angeles main line. Note the small mesa on the horizon above the 102. This is the same mesa visible in the top photo. *Above: Joe McMillan; below: Mel Finzer.*

The scenic Curtis Hill area stretches from the Cimarron River west to Curtis, a distance of about 16 miles. After crossing the river, the tracks climb 550 feet on a curvy right of way to reach more characteristic flatlands west of Curtis. The area abounds in excellent photo locations and is a favorite spot for photographers. Vehicle access is limited in some areas, but there are enough photo locations from county roads to make a visit worthwhile. To get to the scenic areas, turn north off of U. S. Highway 412 (formerly Oklahoma Route 15) onto the paved county road leading to Quinlan. (This junction is 17.5 miles east of Woodward on U. S. 412.) The county road passes over the main line at mile 363 at what is probably the best photo location of the area. The road leads into Quinlan and generally follows the railroad northeast of there. Bearing right at the fork will bring you to another overpass. This structure crosses the rails at mile 359.6, which is another fine location for the photographer. Following the road east, then north will bring you to the east end of Belva siding. A gravel road leading north off the pavement east of Belva will take you under the main line at mile 354.2, which is in the middle of the big curve mentioned on the previous page (curve No. 41 in the engineering records). Some hiking might be necessary here to find a favorable photo spot. Continuing north on the gravel road will take you to Heman siding at mile 352. Visitors might find maps of Woodward, Major and Woods Counties helpful.

Above . . . Merger-painted C30-7 8141 leads train 189 (Chicago-Richmond) around curve No. 41 just east of Belva at mile 355. It's 4:51 p.m. on December 21, 1988. In June 1978 . . . *bottom right* . . . clean F45s 5919 and 5904 (now 5969 and 5954) drift down a 0.6% grade on curve 41 as they speed mixed manifest east. The mesa shown at the left of the 8141 in the photo above is the same one appearing above the 5919 in this view. (Veteran photographer Preston George immortalized this curve in 1946 with his photographs of Santa Fe steam.) Top right . . . "Yellowbonnet" F7A 331 pilots an eastbound mainline local just east of Belva on April 12, 1975. Fourteen former red and silver warbonnet F7 cabs were painted into this scheme in the early 1970s when they were permanently reassigned to freight duties. No. 331, fomerly the 43C, was rebuilt to CF7 2444 in August 1977. *Above: Joe McMillan; two photos right page: Lee Berglund.*

Belva, named for the daughter of a Santa Fe section foreman, is a 11,804-foot siding 10 miles west of Waynoka. *Top left* . . . SF30C 9546 winds around curves at the east end of Belva on August 8, 1987. The engines and first few cars of the eastbound manifest are leaning into curve 41. *Bottom left* . . . A little hiking is necessary to photograph the west end of Belva siding. At 5:58 p.m. the next afternoon, westbound 337 eases out of the siding and accelerates up the 1% grade toward Quinlan. The mixed freight has just met train 678, an eastbound BN run-through which passed this spot 17 minutes earlier. *Above* . . . Quinlan is 5.3 miles west of Belva. This is single track, CTC-signalled territory and dispatchers frequently use both sidings to stage meets. In November 1985, black skies dominate the scene as a westbound curves into town behind SD40 5014 and three EMD mates. *Below* . . . Caterpillar-engined SD45-2 5855 leads train 308 around a mile-long curve at Quinlan. It's 4:15 p.m., August 16, 1989. The siding is just visible below the grain elevator. *Two photos left page and below: Joe McMillan; above: Kenneth B. Fitzgerald.*

The main line and siding at Quinlan have separate rights of way. Prior to a line relocation project in 1945 and 1946, the siding was the main track. *Top left* . . . On August 9, 1987, the 891 train zips under the rural road connecting Quinlan with U. S. Highway 412—one mile to the left. The track at the left of the train is the west end of the siding. *Above* . . . From the overpass at 8:05 p.m. the previous evening, the long lens records train 348 halted near the west end of the siding, its crew waiting for a proceed signal as the rear end of an eastbound passes by in the siding. *Below* . . . On October 5, 1982, freshly remanufactured SD45 5337 strings through the siding where it will be passed momentarily by the 2nd 188. From a hilltop located in between the main track and siding just west of mile 362 . . . *bottom left* . . . BN-AT&SF run-through train 698 rounds a 75 degree curve. The siding is located at right; note the signal. *Two photos left page and above: Joe McMillan; below: Michael W. Blaszak.*

Top left . . . Far from home sod, Canadian National SD50F 5456 pilots train 891 east at the west end of Quinlan siding on October 21, 1988. The big unit visited the Santa Fe for a month giving railroad officials and employees an opportunity to experience first hand the Canadian-style cab and desk-top control console while the company was formulating plans for its own "comfort cab" GP60Ms and DASH 8-40BWs scheduled for delivery in 1990. Trailing the CN locomotive are three Santa Fe SDFP45s, an ex-Amtrak SDF40-2 and business car *Mountainair*. [For additional information, see pages 20-21, Volume 1.] *Bottom left* . . . GP50 3844 and helpers stir up snow flakes on the main track at the same location in February 1986. *Above* . . . The last few seconds of sunlight illuminate the red soil and reflect off the nose of SD40-2 5114 as it grinds upgade at Quinlan at 8:12 p.m. on August 8, 1989 with train 308. *Top left: Ed Kanak; bottom left: Kenneth B. Fitzgerald; Quinlan antique sign (8-16-89) and above: Joe McMillan.*

Above . . . The low light glints off the side of train 308 as the covered hopper train approaches the mile-long curve west of Quinlan between miles 363 and 364. (This is the same train pictured on the previous page.) *Top right . . .* It's 7:55 a.m., September 27, 1990 as SD45-2 5810 crosses 6th Street in downtown Woodward with eastbound freight. The Woodward station still stands and can be seen to the left of the train in the distance. The rear of the train is crossing the Northwestern Oklahoma Railroad (NOKL), a local switching line using a remnant of M-K-T's old Western Subdivision (Wichita Falls, Texas to Forgan, Oklahoma) to reach several Woodward industries. The rail crossing was removed in November 1991 confining the NOKL to businesses on the north side of the Santa Fe. The grain elevator at right is served by both the Santa Fe and NOKL. *Bottom right . . .* Gerlach (GER-lack), mile 386.3, is the first siding west of Woodward. A rural overpass (Santa Fe bridge 386.9) near the west end of the siding is a nice spot to view trains. On August 8, 1987, SF30C 9546 wheels eastbound freight while the Waynoka-Amarillo local waits in the siding. *Above and bottom right: Joe McMillan; top right: David P. Oroszi.*

214

Above . . . Eastbound piggybacker 891 leans into the start of a 92 degree curve at Gerlach. The track at left is the siding and the track diverging from it serves a large fertilizer plant. This photo was taken from bridge 386.9 at 5:36 p.m. on August 15, 1989. *Top right* . . . Tangier, Oklahoma is located at mile 392.6, 6.3 miles west of Gerlach. There are three rural overpasses here: at miles 390.5, 391.3 and 392.4. The latter offers the best vantage point as one can view the east end of the 8,164-foot Tangier siding. At 6:15 p.m. the same day, train 813 pulls out of the old house track after picking up a mis-directed car set out by a westbound train a few hours earlier. In a few minutes, the train will recouple, conduct an air test and move out of the siding toward Waynoka. *Bottom right* . . . GP38 2321 shoves Jordan spreader 199255 along the main track west of Fargo, Oklahoma on August 9, 1989. *Three photos: Joe McMillan.*

From here, main line rails continue west through Shattuck to the Texas state line at mile 427.7 near Higgins. [Volume 3 of the Santa Fe in Color Series will cover Shattuck, the Shattuck Subdivision and the main line west to Amarillo and beyond.] We now leave the Panhandle Subdivision and jump to Wichita, Kansas to begin the final leg of our journey.

The remainder of our photographic tour covers the Santa Fe main line from Wichita south through Arkansas City and Oklahoma City to the Texas state line north of Gainesville, along with the Oklahoma branches.

Top and middle left . . . The Sunflower State Operation Lifesaver Special pulls into Wichita on April 8, 1986 to be interchanged to the Missouri Pacific for the next day's trip. The special had originated earlier that day in Kansas City and had stopped at Topeka, Emporia, Newton (see page 58) and North Wichita to promote grade crossing safety. Tomorrow, the train will leave Wichita and run east over the MoPac to El Dorado, then north to McPherson where it will be interchanged to the Union Pacific for Salina and the return to Kansas City. *Above* . . . There are several photo opportunities in Winfield, Kansas, but the complicated trackage in and around the town can be confusing. Train 185 (Chicago-Dallas) crosses the Walnut River—one of four crossings in Winfield—on Ark City Sub bridge 250.2. Super Fleet SDFP45s 106-103-102 add color to the head end on a snowy day in February 1990. The left track is the Ark City Sub siding. *Below* . . . On a better day two years prior, SD45-2 5831 leads train 305 (Kansas City-Silsbee, Texas) over the same bridge. In less than two miles the train will cross the river again. Note the dike on both sides of the right of way. When a flood is imminent, large metal gates are placed across the tracks to contain the flood waters. Southward trains are then detoured west to Kiowa and down the Enid Sub to Guthrie where they rejoin the Oklahoma Sub. *Bottom left* . . . An audience gathers in front of the Arkansas City station as a Wichita bound Ringling Brothers Barnum and Bailey Circus train pulls to a halt for a crew change. Until mid-1965, Ark City was headquarters for the Oklahoma Division. When the division dissolved, its trackage went to the Middle and Eastern Divisions. *Top and middle left: Joe McMillan; bottom left and above: Fred Tefft; below: Keel Middleton.*

The Oklahoma Subdivision of the Southern Region stretches 259.4 miles from Arkansas City south to Gainesville, Texas. For many years, the northern two thirds of this line (Arkansas City to Purcell) belonged to the Oklahoma Division (later Middle Division) of the Eastern Lines, while the southern segment was part of the Northern Division of the Gulf (later Western) Lines. On May 21, 1989, the territory was consolidated and became the Oklahoma Subdivision of the Kansas Division. In the restructuring of August 15, 1990, the line was assigned to the Southern Region. *Top right* . . . The 5364-3655-2120-2887-8030 (SD45/GP39-2/GP7/GP35/C30-7) exit the siding at Hackney, Kansas, 7.3 miles north of Ark City, with southbound freight. The photo was taken at 2:40 p.m. on September 23, 1989 from the old U. S. Highway 77 overpass, mile 256.7. There's more to Hackney than what is apparent in the photo. An industrial lead diverges from the six-car run-around track, visible at the left of the train, and runs west to serve several businesses. There is also a track serving the Hackney Farmers Union Co-op grain elevator seen in the distance. *Bottom right* . . . F7A 259, a CF7 and a GP7 move mixed freight south near mile 267, just out of Arkansas City. The Kansas-Oklahoma border is about a mile ahead of the train. *Above* . . . Ponca City, built on "oil, soil and toil," is 25.5 miles south of Arkansas City. The city is dominated by a large Conoco refinery and is an important Santa Fe location. GP38 3513 and GP7 2198 idle across from the station on October 7, 1983, as they await the second trick crew that will return them to their switching assignment at the Conoco refinery a short distance to the south. *Above: Michael W. Blaszak; top right: David P. Oroszi; bottom right: Lee Berglund.*

For many years, the Santa Fe operated a number of branch lines east of the present Oklahoma Subdivision. One of these lines, considered more of a secondary main line than a branch, left the Arkansas City-Gainesville main track at Newkirk, Oklahoma, 12.4 miles south of Ark City, and ran south paralleling the main track to Pauls Valley. The line between Newkirk and Shawnee was operated as the Second District of the Oklahoma Division (later Cushing District of the Middle Division), while the segment between Shawnee and Pauls Valley was designated as the Pauls Valley District of the Northern Division. The 184-mile line was built in 1903 and 1904 as the Eastern Oklahoma Railway and served area farm lands and oil fields for many years until abandoned in stages between 1963 and 1985. There were several other lines in the region, all of which have been abandoned. [See back end sheets.]

Aside from some industrial trackage in Shawnee, all that remained of the Cushing District by the middle of 1983 was a 44.8-mile segment between Fairfax and Cushing. Access to the orphaned line was gained over Burlington Northern's Tulsa-Enid-Avard line from Black Bear, on the AT&SF main line, to Camp. *Bottom left . . .* GP20 3036 guides the Cushing District local around the connecting track from the BN to the Cushing District main track at Camp at 11:53 a.m. on October 28, 1983. *Above . . .* In July 1983, the 3041 switches the Cushing Rail Car facility north of Cushing. Cushing Rail Car leased the 24-mile line on January 1, 1985—after Santa Fe had abandoned it the previous year—and operated it until April 1989 as the Cimarron River Valley Railway. It was later abandoned. *Below . . .* On July 19, 1983, the local crosses the Arkansas River north of Ralston while returning to Camp from Fairfax. *Top left . . .* The 24.4-mile Stillwater Subdivision is another branch orphaned by abandonments. The line is served by local LSA02 which originates at Ark City, runs south to Black Bear, then over the BN to Pawnee where it diverges for Stillwater. On October 26, 1983, GP38 3526 hustles the Stillwater local west on the BN toward Black Bear. *Two photos left page: Michael W. Blaszak; two photos this page: Joe McMillan.*

Guthrie is located on the main line at mile 352.6, 31.3 miles north of Oklahoma City. The town, named for a director of the Santa Fe, was the capital of Oklahoma Territory and of the State of Oklahoma until June 1910 when the seat of state government was moved to Oklahoma City. *Above*... Train 315 passes Guthrie's attractive station at 5:20 p.m. on September 22, 1989 on its way south to Oklahoma City. The station, built in 1902 and 1903, still stands in 1991. *Below*... Noble Avenue passes over the main line just north of the depot. From that location, the camera records the passing of northbound freight behind a pair of GE U36Cs on June 10, 1980. The track at the left of the train is the Guthrie siding while the track to the right leads to the Enid District main line. The Enid District swings away from the main behind the photographer and heads northwest to Enid and Kiowa. *Above: David P. Oroszi; below: Kenneth B. Fitzgerald.*

Above . . . Southbound train 185 disturbs the birds as it curves through the old passenger station at Oklahoma City on the north main track in December 1988. GP7 switcher 2143 paces the auto parts train on the south main. There are two main tracks through here, part signalled ABS (automatic block) and part CTC (centralized traffic control). At this point, the trains are in ABS "rule 94" territory, which Santa Fe rules instructors term a "no man's land." In this section, trains may use the main tracks in either direction, but must travel at restricted speed. There is no superiority of trains and all traffic passing through must watch out for all other traffic and be governed accordingly. For obvious reasons, rule 94 territory is not common and is found only in certain congested areas. *Above: Frank D. Frisch.*

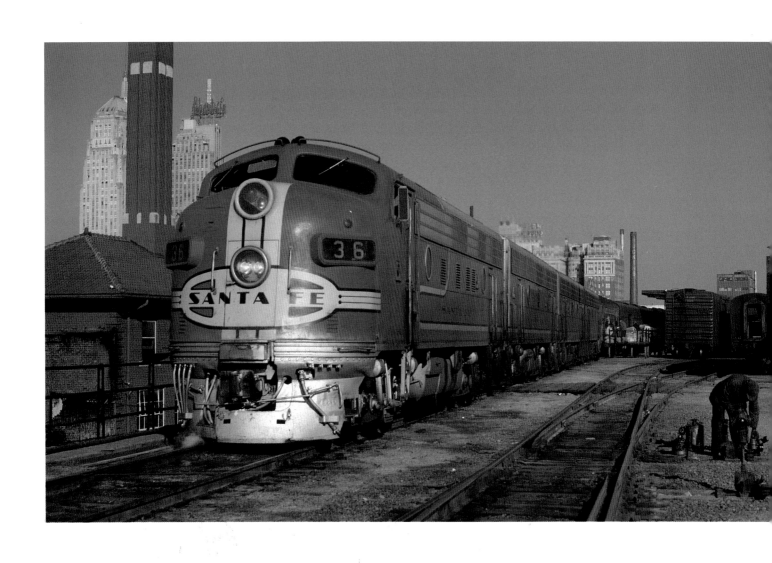

Top left . . . Santa Fe's *Texas Chief* (Chicago-Houston) makes a regular station stop at Oklahoma City on Christmas Eve 1964. No. 15 was due to depart at 8:55 a.m. after a ten minute stop. (Note the sectionman at right refueling kerosene switch lamps.) *Bottom left . . .* Eleven years later, the Oklahoma City skyline has changed, and so has the train. Amtrak's *Lone Star* pauses before continuing south. It was scheduled out at 9:25 a.m. and into Houston at 8:45 that evening. Amtrak assumed this service on May 1, 1971 and operated the train (with a May 1974 name change to *Lone Star*) until it was discontinued in October 1979.

For many years, Nowers Yard, located about three miles north of the passenger station, was Santa Fe's principal freight yard in Oklahoma City. In 1980, the company opened Flynn Yard, a new facility seven miles south of the station. Flynn supports a huge General Motors assembly plant located at the end of a five-mile, double track industrial spur. The spur leads east off the main line from a wye at the north end of Flynn Yard. *Above . . .* SDF45 5986 and SD45 5406 idle away the night hours at the GM plant on September 21, 1989. In a few hours, the units will power train 433 to Kansas City. (Train V-OKKC has since replaced this symbol.) Note the modern yard office and tower. *Below . . .* In August 1988, a pair of GP7 slug sets (1315-118 and 1313-116) occupy both main switching leads into the GM plant. The 1313 has 22 cars for Flynn while the 1315 shuffles tri-levels. There are normally three or four slug sets assigned to Oklahoma City. *Top left: Joe McMillan; bottom left: Kenneth B. Fitzgerald; above and below: Frank D. Frisch.*

The Santa Fe serves Shawnee, 37 miles east of Oklahoma City, by way of trackage rights over Union Pacific's Shawnee Branch. (This was formerly M-K-T's Oklahoma Subdivision, and prior to that, Rock Island's Subdivision 33, a portion of the Memphis-Oklahoma City-Amarillo-Tucumcari Choctaw Route.) Until 1970, Santa Fe reached Shawnee from Oklahoma City over its own line acquired with the September 1964 purchase of the Oklahoma City-Ada-Atoka Railway, a 104.4-mile short line running southeast from Oklahoma City to Tupelo. The Santa Fe abandoned the Oklahoma City-Shawnee portion of the OCAA (except for a small segment in Midwest City now used as an industrial spur) after trackage rights over the CRI&P were secured. (The Shawnee-Tupelo segment of the OCAA was abandoned in two parts by June 1982.) *Above* . . . The Shawnee local, then symbolled LMI59, approaches the Santa Fe at Oklahoma City on 10 m.p.h. UP track behind GP7s 2140 and 2143 on December 6, 1988. *Below* . . . A year later, the Shawnee local leaves the small Union Pacific yard at Harter and is about to request permission from the Santa Fe dispatcher at Newton, Kansas to enter the main track for the run south to Flynn Yard. Today, locals LSA04 and LSA05 serve Shawnee on an over-one-day-and-back-the-next schedule. *Both photos: Frank D. Frisch.*

On pages 222 and 223, we mentioned that Shawnee was also on Santa Fe's secondary main line which ran south from Newkirk through Cushing and Shawnee to Pauls Valley. By the late 1970s, only a portion of the line remained in Shawnee to serve local industries. Shawnee Milling—located off the old OCAA main track—and a Mobil chemical plant are Santa Fe's primary customers here. *Above* . . . Certainly one of the most distinctive stations on the Santa Fe is this unique structure at Shawnee. In the late 1970s, Santa Fe relocated its offices to a former lumber yard a few blocks north, but happily the castle-like building survives in 1991. *Below* . . . The Shawnee local switches on the main track in front of the station on August 8, 1978. *Above: Jim Primm; below: Joe McMillan.*

Above . . . A summer thunderstorm brews in the north as merger-red SD45-2 5814 and SD40 5001 idle in the siding at Flynn Yard on August 1, 1989 at the point of train 185 (Chicago-Dallas). The train had just set out its Oklahoma City pigs and auto parts cars and now waits as a switcher attaches a rear-end fill to the train. The track to the left of the train is the Oklahoma Subdivision main line. *Below* . . . Seven GP7s get a roll on a southbound grain train leaving Flynn on March 12, 1988. Although the Geeps are working hard, most of the smoke in this scene is from a large grass fire. The train is leaving the siding and passing over Northeast 27th Street at the very south end of Flynn Yard. Incredibly, Santa Fe's GP7s have been on the property for forty years. No other diesel locomotives have served the company so long. They were delivered between 1950 and 1953 and were responsible for sending hundreds of steam engines to scrap. The units were remanufactured between 1972 and 1981 and emerged from shopping in three class groups: 1310-1329, 2000-2027 and 2050-2243. In late 1991, 65% of the original fleet was still on the roster. The company has been selling GP7s to short lines and scrap dealers for several years and will continue to do so until the class is gone. While most of the remaining Geeps are assigned to yards and locals, some can still be seen on main line secondary freights. *Above and below: Frank D. Frisch.*

Norman, Oklahoma, home of the University of Oklahoma, is located 18 miles south of Oklahoma City. Named for Abner Norman, a Santa Fe surveyor, it is the state's third largest city. *Above* . . . On October 20, 1974, four dented and tired old workhorses rumble pass Norman's attractive brick station with southbound mixed freight. In less than four years, lead unit 252C would be rebuilt to CF7 2421 at Cleburne (KLEE-burn) Shops south of Fort Worth (now closed). In 1984, the 2421 was sold to the Blue Mountain and Reading in Pennsylvania, and then to the Black River & Western Railroad at Ringoes, New Jersey where it was renumbered 42. The station, built in 1909, was presented to the city in November 1987. *Below* . . . Amtrak No. 15, the southbound *Lone Star*, accelerates from a station stop at Norman on a frosty morning in February 1978. In less than two years, the *Lone Star* would be discontinued, leaving Oklahoma without rail passenger service. Also gone from this scene is class Ce-1 caboose 999279 and the trio of CF7s at right. *Above and below: Kenneth B. Fitzgerald.*

Our southward journey brings us next to Purcell at mile 417.3, or 517.5 if you are heading north. It was here on April 26, 1887 that the Gulf, Colorado & Santa Fe (GC&SF) met the Southern Kansas Railway to form a continuous AT&SF route from Kansas City to Galveston, Texas. We will cover the GC&SF in greater detail in Volume 3 of the Santa Fe in Color Series, but briefly, the "GC" was organized in 1875 by Galveston businessmen who intended to construct a line to Santa Fe, New Mexico. However, by May 15, 1886, when Santa Fe assumed control of the GC&SF, the company had built a main line north from the Gulf to Fort Worth, with branches from Cleburne to Dallas and from Temple to Coleman. There was also a line linking Somerville with Conroe in east Texas. Under Santa Fe control, the railway was rapidly pushed north from Fort Worth to join the company's Southern Kansas Railway building south from Arkansas City. For most of the company's history, Purcell was a crew change point between the Northern Division of the Gulf (later Western) Lines and the Middle Division of the Eastern Lines. In October 1972, the Santa Fe and its transportation unions implemented an agreement whereby train and engine crews would run through between Gainesville, Texas and Arkansas City, eliminating the need to change crews at Purcell. (However, some "short pool" crews continued to change there until 1986). *Above* . . . Canadian National units idle at the point of a southbound freight in the Purcell yard on September 29, 1977. Short of power at the time, the Santa Fe had leased a number of CN units to help out. To avoid conflict with the company's own 4000 class SD39s, the Santa Fe temporarily renumbered the 4000 series CN motors to 4100s. (Note the "clean" numeral ones in the number boards.) The bridge in the background carries U.S. Highway 77 across the Canadian River, main line and yard. *Below* . . . An A-B-A set of F-units pauses for a crew change at Purcell on April 1, 1973 with northbound freight. The lead unit sports the "bluebonnet" paint scheme applied to seven former red and silver passenger units after they were permanently reassigned from Amtrak passenger service to freight duties following the arrival of Amtrak's new SDP40Fs. *Above: Kenneth B. Fitzgerald; below: Jim Primm.*

Pauls Valley, Oklahoma is 21.9 miles south of Purcell. The 23.9-mile Lindsay District branched off the main line here and ran northwest along the Washita (wash-i-TAW) River to Lindsay. The line opened in December 1903 as the Kiowa, Chickasha and Fort Smith Railway. It was purchased by the Eastern Oklahoma Railway in 1904, which in turn was acquired by the Santa Fe in June 1907. For years, Lindsay was world famous for its broomcorn; its stiff-branched tops were used in making brooms and brushes. Unitil it was abandoned in 1985, the Lindsay District was served by local trains 2531 and 2532 which made a Pauls Valley-Lindsay round trip on a tri-weekly schedule. *Left* . . . A unique feature of the Lindsay District was its stone milepost markers. *Bottom* . . . The westbound local passes over a rural road between Pauls Valley and Maysville on October 19, 1977. Later that day . . . *below* . . . the train stops alongside the Lindsay station while the crew plans their work. CF7 2557, built from F7A 302L at Cleburne in August 1973, is in charge of the local today. The 1500 h.p. unit would run almost four more years before being retired in August 1981. *Left: Michael W. Blaszak, below and bottom: Kenneth B. Fitzgerald.*

Below . . . A sunny October 19, 1977 finds southbound train 395 rounding the big curve at mile 498, two miles north of Pauls Valley. In less than a mile, the train will cross the Washita River as it approaches town. On the point are leased CN SD40 5056 (temporarily renumbered 5156 by the Santa Fe) and GE U28CG 7904, a former passenger unit purchased as the 354 in July 1966. As mentioned earlier, a power shortage occurred during the summer of 1977 forcing the Santa Fe to seek help. Forty-five CN GP40s and SD40s, as well as a number of Chicago & North Western units, were leased from June to late fall to alleviate the problem. Most of the CN units were renumbered by the Santa Fe to avoid conflicts with AT&SF engines. *Top left* . . . Amtrak No. 16, the northbound *Lone Star*, pauses at Pauls Valley on August 17, 1974. *Bottom left* . . . Vegetation control has always been a big part of each year's maintenance of way activities. The Vegetation Control Department, located at Albuquerque, maintained several spray trains that annually toured the railroad spreading weed chemicals along the right of way. The spray trains have since been sold and the company currently contracts vegetation control activities. At 3:49 p.m., May 11, 1984, spray car 199205 approaches a county road overpass at mile 476, two miles south of Davis, Oklahoma. [For more spray train photos, see Volume 1, pages 106-108.] *Below and top left: Kenneth B. Fitzgerald; bottom left: Michael W. Blaszak.*

For about 25 miles, from Davis to Ardmore, main line rails wind along the Washita River through the rugged and picturesque Arbuckle Mountains. There are many photo opportunities in the area, but one may have to do a little hiking to find the best spots. *Above* . . . GP39-2 3647 and mates string southbound freight along the Washita at mile 474, just north of Rayford, on May 19, 1976. Trains are restricted to 50 m.p.h. through here, but that's fast enough to kick up dust from freshly placed ballast. *Top right* . . . Three years later, on September 23, 1979, a pair of GE U36Cs guide southbound train 325 around the 79 degree curve at Crusher, mile 465.7, home to a large Dolese Bros. limestone quarry, crusher (hence the station name) and loading point. (This facility has since closed.) Today, most limestone from the area is loaded at Western Rock Products in nearby Davis. *Bottom right* . . . On the same day, GP38 3541 leads southbound hoppers around the curve south of Crusher between miles 465 and 466. The south switch to the limestone plant—since removed—is hidden by the front portion of the train. *Three photos: Kenneth B. Fitzgerald.*

Bridge 464.3 (between Crusher and Gene Autry) carries the main track over the Washita River and into Carter County. The Washita flows southeast from here into Lake Texoma while the main line angles southwest toward Ardmore. *Above* . . . A high bluff on the south side of the river provides a great vantage point to view the 305 train as it moves south toward Texas on January 4, 1986. *Below* . . . Five years earlier, in April 1981, GP38 3549 (now numbered 2349) rolls a southbound grain train over the same bridge. *Bottom right* . . . The camera looks upsteam earlier that day as three GEs and an EMD cross the Washita with more grain.

From the Washita River crossing, southbound trains negotiate five 35 m.p.h. curves before passing through Gene Autry at mile 460.4. The town, named for the famous western movie star, had a propensity for changing its name. It was originally called Lou, then it became Dresden and then Berwyn. On November 16, 1941, amid great celebration and hoopla, the town was renamed Gene Autry. (The movie star had purchased a 1,360-acre ranch nearby.) Riding to the cheers of 35-40,000 people that day, two cowboys "rode down the right of way in dead heat, lassoed the Berwyn [station] sign, then turned and made off, jerking the wooden plaque to the ground. Santa Fe workmen then erected a much larger sign on two posts, bearing the words Gene Autry, and as a climax Gene rode under the sign waving his five-gallon hat to the crowd." The Santa Fe had played a big part in the celebration by shuttling celebrants back and forth between Ardmore and Gene Autry, 9.9 miles. Gene, incidentally, worked as a telegrapher for four railroads (the Santa Fe wasn't one of them) before beginning his movie career. *Above . . .* Gene Autry was somewhat quieter thirty-four years later as No. 16, the *Lone Star*, zooms by a freight sitting in the siding behind a pair of GP39-2s. *Top left: John Leopard; bottom left and below: Jim Primm; above: Kenneth B. Fitzgerald.*

Ardmore, located on the "Sunny Side of the Arbuckle Mountains" is a modern industrial city whose roots are deep in oil and agriculture. *Above* . . . Ardmore's beautiful depot, built in 1917 and remodeled in 1960, was photographed on February 15, 1980. The thirty-mile Ringling District ran west from Ardmore to Healdton and Ringling. It was built as the Oklahoma, New Mexico and Pacific in 1913 and 1914 and obviously had big ideas about where it was headed. The railroad became part of the Santa Fe in 1926 and was abandoned in 1976. A portion of the branch remains in Ardmore as an industrial lead to a Uni-Royal Goodrich tire plant and other businesses.

Thirty-two miles south of Ardmore, at mile 418.3, six 200-foot through trusses carry the Santa Fe across the famed Red River into Texas. *Below* . . . On February 4, 1990, train 513 scoots over the river with northbound freight behind a set of three SDFP45s led by the 106. Our journey ends here on the doorstep of the Lone Star State. Volume 3 of the Santa Fe in Color Series will begin in Gainesville, seven miles south of the river and it will cover the AT&SF in Texas, Louisiana and New Mexico. Until then, so long, pardner! *Two photos above: Kenneth B. Fitzgerald; below: Mark R. Lynn.* **End.**

S A N T A   F E
Wheat Lines . . .

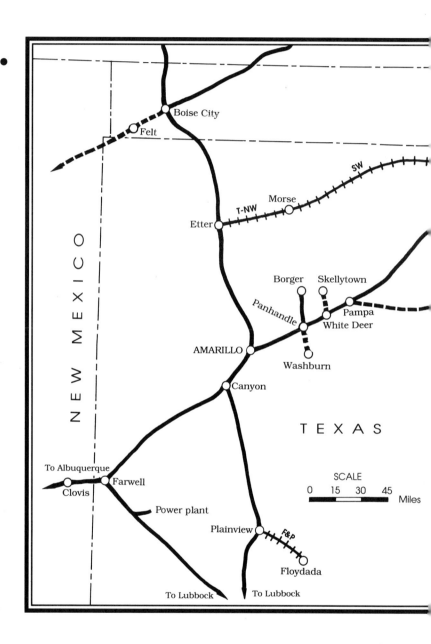

——————	Lines currently operated by Santa Fe
- - - - - -	Lines abandoned by Santa Fe
•••••••• **(UP)**	Santa Fe trackage rights (host railroad in parenthesis)
+++++++ **GCN**	Former-Santa Fe line operated by regional/shortline carrier
+++++++ **KCTV**	Former-Santa Fe line abandoned by regional/shortline carrier

NEW MEXICO

TEXAS

Boise City

Felt

SW

Morse

T-NW

Etter

Borger   Skellytown

Panhandle

Pampa

White Deer

AMARILLO

Washburn

Canyon

To Albuquerque

Farwell

Clovis

Power plant

Plainview   F&P

Floydada

To Lubbock   To Lubbock

SCALE

0   15   30   45   Miles